Also by Christopher Benfey

EMILY DICKINSON AND
THE PROBLEM OF OTHERS

Emily Dickinson

The Dickinson children—Emily, Austin, and Lavinia—painted by O.S. Ballard, 1840.

Emily Dickinson

Lives of a Poet

Christopher Benfey

George Braziller
New York

For Mickey

*"The purpose of poetry is to remind us
how difficult it is to remain just one person,
for our house is open, there are no keys in the doors,
and invisible guests come in and out at will."*

Czeslaw Milosz

Contents

Preface

Emily Dickinson died on May 15, 1886. Her self-appointed literary executors were faced with two difficulties one might call cosmetic. One was the look of the poems, the other the look of the poet. The first problem was easily taken care of, and Lavinia Dickinson, the poet's younger sister, was lucky in her choice of editors for the first selection of Dickinson's poems. Mabel Loomis Todd, who was having an affair with Dickinson's brother, was a clever critic and gifted painter. If she had not been so convinced of the value of the poems, we might well not have them today, for only seven had been published during Dickinson's life, all anonymously and none with her complete approval. Thomas Wentworth Higginson was a professional man of letters whose advice Dickinson had sought in the 1860s. Todd and Higginson knew exactly what would appeal to readers in the 1890s. They fixed rhymes, diction, punctuation, spelling, meter until the poems looked like, and sometimes sounded like, genteel magazine verse of the late nineteenth century.

But while the editors had nearly two thousand poems to choose from, they had only one photograph. Higginson had asked for a portrait twenty-four years earlier, and Dickinson had told him she had none. "I noticed the quick wore off those things, in a few days," she wrote, and added, "I am small, like the Wren, and my Hair is bold, like the Chestnut Bur—and my eyes, like the Sherry in the Glass, that the Guest leaves—Would

The daguerreotype, 1848.

The retouched daguerreotype,
as it appeared in 1924.

this do just as well?" When she was fourteen Dickinson had written her friend, Abiah Root: "I am growing handsome very fast indeed! I expect I shall be the belle of Amherst when I reach my 17th year." It happens that the familiar daguerreotype of Emily Dickinson, the only photographic image we have, was taken when the poet was seventeen.

There was general agreement that the daguerreotype was disappointing. As Mabel Loomis Todd's daughter later remarked, "Both brother and sister objected to it on the ground that it made her look too plain." Lavinia claimed that her sister wore her hair looped over her ears and knotted in back, "because it was the way Elizabeth Barrett Browning did," and she had seen a portrait of a cousin of the Dickinsons wearing a white lace ruff at the neck, a style she thought would suit Emily. There followed several months of doctoring, retouching, and "improving" the daguerreotype. The image of Dickinson in lace ruff and curled hair was first used in 1924 (the editors of the 1890s had finally decided against it), and some poetry anthologies still carry it, just as they still sometimes include the "improved" versions of the poems.

Why do we care what poets look like? Perhaps we have a vestigial belief in the science of physiognomy, by which the inner springs of the soul are detected from the contours of the face. (Think of W. H. Auden's "italic face," to borrow a phrase from Dickinson; in his last years, his own poems seemed somehow inscribed on it.) Or perhaps the face gives an illusion of solidity to the words, and a body to the voice. As Dickinson wrote, "A Letter always feels to me like immortality because it is the mind alone without corporeal friend."

Dickinson herself, in any case, cared a great deal about what writers looked like. She had portraits of Thomas Carlyle, Elizabeth Barrett Browning, and George Eliot on her bedroom wall, and sent pictures of Barrett Browning to several of her

13

THREE VERSIONS OF
"THE SOUL SELECTS HER OWN SOCIETY"

The manuscript, with alternate words at the bottom of the page.

26   *POEMS.*

XIII.

EXCLUSION.

THE soul selects her own society,
    Then shuts the door ;
On her divine majority
Obtrude no more.

Unmoved, she notes the chariot's pausing
At her low gate ;
Unmoved, an emperor is kneeling
Upon her mat.

I 've known her from an ample nation
Choose one ;
Then close the valves of her attention
Like stone.

*From the 1890 edition
of* Poems.

The Soul selects her own Society—
Then—shuts the Door—
To her divine Majority—
Present no more—

Unmoved—she notes the Chariots—pausing—
At her low Gate—
Unmoved—an Emperor be kneeling
Upon her Mat—

I've known her—from an ample nation—
Choose One—
Then—close the Valves of her attention—
Like Stone—

*The restored
version, published
in 1955.*

friends. She worried that Lavinia would be disappointed by a likeness of George Eliot she was expecting: "I wince in perspective," she wrote, "lest it be no more sweet. God chooses repellant settings, don't he, for his best Gems?"

It has taken many years to restore Dickinson's "settings," and today we find the cosmetic adjustments far more repellant than what they were meant to improve. We have to admit finally that we simply don't know what she looked like as an adult. Meanwhile we should be grateful that so many of her manuscripts were preserved. It is a starker, more idiosyncratic poet that emerges from these; she is more fragmentary in her utterance, more wayward in her punctuation, diction, and spelling. As the authority of her imagination becomes clearer the notion that we could improve her poetry seems more and more ludicrous. She has completed her work, and we must learn to read her.

Introduction

Despite the attention she has received, Emily Dickinson remains almost as mysterious as Shakespeare. Some of her poems are so familiar that we quote them without knowing we are doing so: "The Soul selects her own Society"; "I'm Nobody! Who are you? Are you—Nobody—Too?"; "Success is counted sweetest by those who ne'er succeed"; "Parting is all we know of heaven, and all we need of hell." Such lines have entered our language with some of the anonymous authority of proverbs. No other American poet, not Whitman or Frost or Sandburg, has such currency. But the many books and essays about her, good and bad, don't penetrate the mystery of her life. Her riddling words about nature could be about herself:

> To pity those that know her not
> Is helped by the regret
> That those who know her, know her less
> The nearer her they get.

She is part of our language without quite being part of our history, despite constant efforts to claim her for one tradition or another. Thus she is seen as the "last flower of American Puritanism"; the first American modernist; a poet of the Civil War; a nineteenth-century female poet; a Romantic or lesbian or Symbolist poet. And yet, there is little that would qualify as literary debate about her work. Dickinson criticism hasn't reached that stage. It seems, on the contrary, to be continually beginning. A specious air of discovery, of clues and solutions, is present in much of the criticism and biography. Her lover, we are assured, has been identified at last. Or we are told that the correct order of the poems has finally been established, her debt to this or that author conclusively demonstrated.

It is as though the very weight of the material holds out the promise of discovery. The Dickinson scholar must be at home in ten enormous books: three volumes of her poems, with variants; three volumes of letters; two volumes of documents, assembled by Jay Leyda, concerning her life and times; and two volumes of biography by Richard Sewall. More than seventeen hundred short poems, without obvious pattern or progression, without titles or dates, challenge the critic to locate the hidden "figure in the carpet." A recent critic affirms that "it is still far too early in the history of Dickinson criticism to declare that there is . . . no mega-motif that makes the whole comprehensible." When, one wonders, will it be late enough? Dickinson herself seems to taunt those who seek an overarching design in her poetry:

> Finding is the first Act
> The second, loss,
> Third, Expedition for
> The "Golden Fleece"
>
> Fourth, no Discovery—
> Fifth, no Crew—
> Finally, no Golden Fleece—
> Jason—sham—too.

The pattern of her life is just as elusive. She baffles the biographer at almost every important moment, except her birth and her death. Emily Dickinson's biographers, to an extent equaled by those of few other poets, are often forced to be educated guessers. In his book *The Years and Hours of Emily Dickinson* (1960) Jay Leyda accurately remarks that "most of our biggest questions about her must remain unanswered." Dickinson, who loved riddles, knew the allure of such a life: "The Riddle we can guess/We speedily despise," she wrote.

What do we most want to know about a poet's life? Samuel Johnson knew, and Emerson knew, though they had very different ideas about what was essential. ("Shakespeare is the only biographer of Shakespeare," Emerson maintained, in *Representative Men*, thus dismissing biographical speculation altogether.) Their accounts of poets were short, incisive, confident. But we, with our gigantic lives in one or two volumes, are less certain.

Legends and myths surround poets about whom little is known, and biography is often seen as an effort to put such myths to rest. Dickinson's chroniclers have had to deal with a pervasive, sentimentalized view of her that is largely traceable to her niece, Martha Dickinson Bianchi. Bianchi published several books in the first half of this century in which she collected poems, letters, and biographical innuendo. She was fond of such characterizations as "She had the soul of a monk of the Middle Ages bound up in the flesh of Puritan descent." She pretended to more knowledge than she had concerning Dickinson's mysterious lover.

Certainly in that first witchery of an undreamed Southern springtime Emily was overtaken—doomed once and forever by her own heart. It was instantaneous, overwhelming, impossible. There is no doubt that two predestined souls were kept apart only by their high sense of duty, and the necessity for preserving love untarnished by the inevitable destruction of another woman's life.

In such words as "certainly" and "there is no doubt" one can detect the rhetoric of fabrication. Bianchi's main purpose seems to have been to present her own mother—Susan Gilbert Dickinson—in the best possible light. This required softening and sentimentalizing the often-strained relations between Susan and her sister-in-law Emily Dickinson. The sentimental version of Dickinson has been enormously hardy. It survives in such popularizations as William Luce's play, "The Belle of Amherst." ("This is my introduction. Black cake. My own special recipe.")

Since so many silly theories about Dickinson have been based on scanty evidence (a recent critic argues, on the basis of textual inference, that she had an abortion in the 1860s), it is tempting to say: We must know everything. This was Jay Leyda's approach, in his fascinating documentary—that is, collection of documents—about Emily Dickinson. Richard Sewall's biography, *The Life of Emily Dickinson* (1974), is based on the same premise. We must know everything, even if, as he writes in his opening sentence, "Almost nothing to do with Emily Dickinson is simple and clear-cut." One reason Sewall's biography is so huge is that he is honest, scrupulous, and skeptical; where an event admits of several interpretations, he discusses them all. Much of Sewall's biography is built up, like a Henry Moore sculpture, by negative space: We don't know much about her life, but if we knew how others saw her, and who these others were, we might get a sense of who she was. Like Leyda he introduces us to the people around Dickinson—although their lives are often as hazy and problematic as her own. Leyda and Sewall wanted to widen the focus, and make us reconsider our assessment of a great poet's life.

Any sketch of Dickinson's life is bound to mislead with confident assertions, but the main facts are these. She was born December 10, 1830, in Amherst, Massachusetts, and died there, of what was diagnosed as Bright's disease, in 1886. She received an excellent education at Amherst Academy, which was founded by, among others, her own grandfather and Noah Webster. It is hard to imagine a closer family than the Dickinsons. The parents were the first to leave the nest: Edward Dickinson died in 1874, his wife Emily Norcross in 1882—and the children remained. Emily's brother Austin married her best friend, Susan Gilbert, in 1856; at the time it was hard to tell whether brother or sister was more in love with her. Edward Dickinson built a house next door, called the Evergreens, for Susan and Austin. Emily and her younger sister Lavinia stayed at home—sewing, baking bread, running the household. ("House is being 'cleaned,'" Emily once wrote, "I prefer pestilence.") They had an Irish maidservant and a man who took care of the horses. Neither sister married.

Emily Dickinson was given her mother's first name and her father's last. Her mother was active in the Amherst community when Emily was young, winning prizes for her cooking and produce at the annual Cattle Show and helping to distribute food to the Amherst poor. She was increasingly an invalid during the last thirty years of her life, however, and she seems a sickly, shadowy figure in many accounts. Emily encouraged this impression; when she was in her forties she liked to pretend, to literary men, that she had had no mother at all. "I never had a mother," she told Thomas Wentworth Higginson. "I suppose a mother is one to whom you hurry when you are troubled." In a sense, Mrs. Dickinson hurried to her, for one of Emily's major occupations in the 1860s and 1870s was taking care of her mother. With the roles reversed her affection grew: "We were never intimate Mother and Children while she was our Mother —but Mines in the same Ground meet by tunneling and when she became our Child, the Affection came."

That she had a father was never in doubt. Edward Dickinson was an imposing figure in Amherst. He comes across in his

Susan Gilbert, about 1851.

Austin, about 1856.

Lavinia, around 1852.

letters as an extremely ambitious man—"a typical success-oriented, work-oriented citizen of expansionist America," in Richard Sewall's characterization. His values seem drawn from the previous century; he promised his wife a life of "rational happiness." In his letter proposing marriage he told her, "My life must be a life of business, of labor and application to the study of my profession." By these standards he was quite successful.

Educated at Amherst College and at Yale, he quickly became

Edward Dickinson, alternatively dated 1853, 1860, and 1874.

the leading lawyer in town. He was for thirty-seven years the treasurer of the college that his father had helped to establish in 1821, and he brought the railroad to Amherst. Dickinson was elected to the General Court of Massachusetts while still in his thirties, and in 1852—when his still unknown daughter was twenty-one—he was elected to the United States Congress, as the representative of the Tenth District of Massachusetts. (He shared an office in Washington with Thomas D. Eliot of New Bedford, grand-uncle of T.S. Eliot.)

But Edward Dickinson seems to have been a remote, austere man who paid for his public success with emotional poverty. Emily observed, probably in the 1860s, "Father says in fugitive moments when he forgets the barrister and lapses into the man, says that his life has been passed in a wilderness, or on an island —of late he says on an island." He had few pleasures, but was passionate about fine horses, which he called "the noblest of all irrational animals."

Relations between father and daughter seem to have been distant; "I am not very well acquainted with father," she once remarked. And yet she maintained toward this morose man an attitude of teasing affection. "He buys me many Books—but begs me not to read them—because he fears they joggle the Mind." For too long he has been regarded as a tyrannical Puritan who blighted his daughter's life. Students of her life in the future will probably come to feel for him the sympathy that Emily Dickinson seems to have increasingly felt. When he died in 1874 he left no will, as though he thought he would live forever.

This was a family obsessed with education. Dickinson's grandfather, Samuel Fowler, lost his wealth and his health in his efforts to establish Amherst College. When the future of the college seemed in doubt, he contributed more money than he could safely part with, left town to take a modest job in the Midwest, and seems to have suffered a general breakdown in health and spirit from which he never fully recovered. Both Dickinson's father and brother served long terms as treasurer of the college and advised its presidents. Austin first chose a teaching career, but after a difficult year teaching Irish boys in Boston gave it up to study law. The major social event of the year in Amherst was Commencement, and prominent visitors always attended the Dickinsons' celebratory teas.

Edward Dickinson believed women should be educated, and sent his daughters to excellent schools. Emily attended Amherst Academy, which drew its young teachers from the college. The curriculum was varied; at fourteen she wrote to a friend, "I have four studies. They are Mental Philosophy, Geology, Latin, and Botany." She then attended Mount Holyoke Female Seminary in South Hadley, the forerunner of the college. Much has been made of her reluctance to participate in the revivals that were staged at the school and in Amherst. "When a Child and Fleeing from Sacrament I could hear the Clergy-man saying 'All who loved the Lord Jesus Christ—were asked to remain'—My flight kept time to the Words." She left Mount Holyoke after a year—we don't know why. Thus, "She was the first major writer of her sex to enjoy access to higher education," as Ellen Moers rightly remarks in *Literary Women*, adding with less justification, "an opportunity she threw away after a single year." By this time Dickinson could educate herself; the breadth of her reading throughout her life does not show the crankiness of an auto-didact, but rather the patient feeding of a cultivated mind.

A sexist bias in the writing of literary history, and a naively positivistic approach to Dickinson's erotic poetry, have resulted in a great deal of speculation about possible lovers. Her family was prominent and she knew, through her father and brother, some of the most interesting men in the area. These included Samuel Bowles, editor of the Springfield newspaper, a batch of

Judge Otis Lord.

clergymen, and, late in her life, Judge Otis Lord of Salem. Every possibility has been scrutinized with an attentiveness worthy of an anxious future mother-in-law. We have hardly taken the same care with the suspected lovers of Walt Whitman, Henry James, or Edgar Allan Poe. But Dickinson is far more interesting than the men she knew, and too often we let them distract us from the real interest of her life. The "critical years" from roughly 1858 to 1862 are remarkable not primarily for some difficulty in her real or imagined love life, but because these are the years when she wrote some of her greatest poetry.

The shape of her life is one of progressive immobility. After a sociable adolescence she restricted her social intercourse more and more to members of her own family, rarely, from the late

1850s on, leaving her house. Finally, in the last years of her life, she would greet visitors from upstairs in her own room, where she could be heard but not seen. There were of course exceptions to this pattern—anomalous appearances downstairs, visits from unexpected friends, and so on; even late in her life she saw those she wanted to see. And yet by 1881 she could say that the postmaster knew who she was "by faith." When she died five years later one of her confidants during the final years, Mabel Loomis Todd, had never seen her face.

Dickinson's attachment to her house is evident in the directions she gave for her own funeral. She requested that the six Irishmen employed by her father to tend the Dickinson grounds carry her coffin. "She asked," as Jay Leyda recounts, "to be carried out the back door, around through the garden, through the opened barn from front to back, and then through the grassy fields to the family plot, always in sight of the house."

But there was no withdrawal of Dickinson's mind or her language, which tended toward an ever more vital mobility. Several of her poems ("They shut me up in Prose," for example) rehearse the relation between physical restriction and the mind's freedom. She loved Byron's "Prisoner of Chillon" for its statement of this theme. "A Prison gets to be a friend," she noted in one of her poems. She seemed to need the safety and rootedness she felt in her own home, and she thought of poetry as a house she lived in—

> I dwell in Possibility—
> A fairer House than Prose—
> More numerous of Windows—
> Superior—for Doors—

She once wrote, in a more gothic mood, "Nature is a Haunted House—but Art—a House that tries to be haunted."

.   .   .

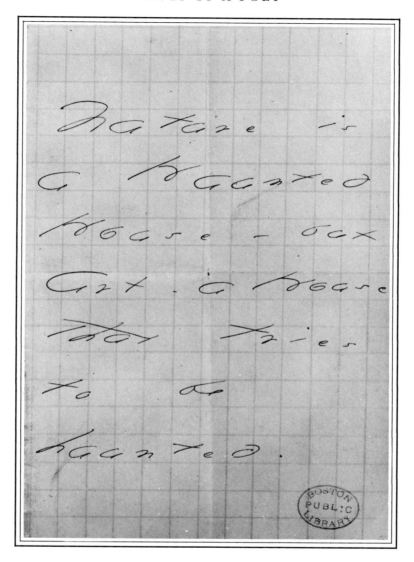

Prose fragment—"Nature is a Haunted House—but Art—a House that tries to be haunted"—included with a letter to Thomas Wentworth Higginson, 1876.

Dickinson's poetry is so rooted in specific places, real and imagined, that what we need is not another history of her life and art but a geography—or, more precisely, a topography—beginning in the house where she was born.

"They say that 'home is where the heart is,'" she once wrote. "I think it is where the *house* is, and the adjacent buildings." Emily Dickinson died in the house in which she was born. The Homestead, as it was called, was built by her grandfather on Main Street in Amherst. It was also called, simply, the Mansion, and the visitor today is struck by its grandeur, and by the care lavished on its fine Greek revival doorway and carved wooden banisters. It was the first house in Amherst built of brick. The Dickinsons, who bought half of the Homestead just before Emily was born, moved to another house, on North Pleasant Street, when she was ten. The earliest sample we have of Emily

Two views of the Homestead, (above and right), from the early part of this century. It remains one of the finest houses in Amherst.

Dickinson's writing is a letter she sent two years later to her brother Austin, who was away at school. It suggests a crowded and confusing set of sleeping arrangements: "I miss my bedfellow very much for it is rare that I can get any now for Aunt Elisabeth is afraid to sleep alone and Vinnie has to sleep with her but I have the privilege of looking under the bed every night which I improve as you might suppose."

The Dickinsons moved back to the Homestead when Emily was twenty-four and her father could afford to buy the entire mansion. The move was the occasion of one of her most interesting letters:

I took at the time a memorandum of my several senses, and also of my hat and coat, and my best shoes—but it was lost in the melee, and I am out with lanterns, looking for myself. . . . It is a kind of *gone-to-Kansas* feeling, and if I sat in a

Amherst town center, after the fire of July 4, 1879. Emily wrote in a letter, "I sprang to the window, and each side of the curtain saw that awful sun. The moon was shining high at the time, and the birds singing like trumpets. Vinnie came soft as a moccasin, 'Don't be afraid, Emily, it is only the fourth of July'. . . . It seemed like a theatre, or a night in London, or perhaps like chaos."

long wagon, with my family tied behind, I should suppose without doubt I was a party of Emigrants!

Thus, they "fulfilled the pantomime contained in the word 'moved'"—an extraordinary outburst of language for what was literally a move around the corner.

Dickinson never got as far as Kansas—though her father once bought a thousand acres in Michigan in a get-rich-quick scheme. She visited Washington and Philadelphia in her twenties, and Boston several times, including two sojourns in her thirties to consult an eye doctor ("eight months of Siberia," she called one of these visits), but that was the sum of her travels. She lived as intensively in one place as Thoreau did. Her brother Austin traveled as far as New Orleans and St. Louis but was unimpressed: "I wouldn't give a volume of Emerson for all the hogs west of the Mississippi." As Emily noted in one of her poems: "We are the birds that stay."

For a long time it was thought that Emily Dickinson was an eccentric recluse in a backward corner of New England who somehow wrote extraordinary poems. For thirty years at least scholars and critics have been contesting that view. Now we know that Amherst in the 1830s and 40s was a sophisticated college town, comparable (and in some cases, as in the wide-spread interest in the natural sciences, superior) to Cambridge, Massachusetts, and that Dickinson's circle of friends included some of the major figures of the time. For us there is an opposite danger, namely, that she will seem an unsurprising and all but inevitable result of her time—precisely the kind of poet that mid-nineteenth-century Amherst should have produced.

Among the many signatures Dickinson used to end her letters was "Amherst," and the town was to some extent an invention of the Dickinsons. Today we might say, with little exaggeration, that what put it on the map was Emily Dickinson's poetry—the most famous building in Amherst is still the Homestead. But three generations of Dickinsons put Amherst on the map in other ways. In the middle of the nineteenth century, when the cities and towns of the United States were increasingly joined together by railroads, the telegraph, and newspapers, the Dickinsons were at the center of these new technologies. Edward Dickinson, the poet's father, led efforts to bring the railroad and the telegraph to Amherst. The Amherst-Belchertown Railroad was completed in 1853, and Edward Dickinson was rewarded for his labors when a locomotive was named for him. One of his daughter's most famous riddle poems, "I like to see it lap the Miles," is inspired by the railroad. Emily's brother Austin dedicated himself to beautifying Amherst. He hired his friend Frederick Law Olmstead, designer of Central Park in New York City, to advise the town on the draining and planting of the common.

Yet Amherst was still a small town. Its population during Dickinson's life barely exceeded three thousand. When she talked of selecting her own society she knew, as far as Amherst was concerned, the company from which she could choose. The economy of Amherst was built around its farms and light industries. Some critics such as Northrop Frye have claimed, probably to emphasize Dickinson's isolation, that Amherst was self-sufficient; but it wasn't. Amherst traded for its needs, and its major export became palm-leaf hats. The Straw Works were just up Main Street from the Dickinson Homestead. Compared to neighboring towns like South Hadley, Amherst's water power was meagre, and the bustling years of its factories and mills had already passed when Dickinson was in her teens. The railroad, meant to stir up a sluggish economy, instead brought more competition to Amherst's factories, and investors in the railroad soon lost their money.

What made Amherst different from neighboring towns in the Connecticut Valley was its intellectual life, centered around the college. But Amherst had a prior intellectual tradition as well. When Dickinson wrote that during her youth, "for several years, my Lexicon—was my only companion," she was in a sense speaking of a neighbor, for Noah Webster, an associate of her grandfather, had come to Amherst in 1812 to write his dictionary.

Amherst had another mark of intellectual distinction. "In the second half of the nineteenth century the village of Amherst," as Jay Leyda notes, "was famous for having more ministers per capita than any other town in the United States." In Amherst the

Sunday sermon had something of the status that we give the Saturday night movie, and Emily Dickinson was an acute sermon critic. ("Sermons on unbelief ever did attract me.") In New England, ministers could assume some of the allure of celebrities, and Dickinson's commentators can be forgiven for often taking too seriously her effusions about certain men of the cloth. Bad preaching, on the other hand, made her indignant: "He preached upon 'Breadth' till it argued him narrow—The Broad was too broad to define."

Amherst preserved the Puritan tradition during a period when Boston had yielded to more liberal tendencies. In what Karl Keller has rightly called "the single most influential essay on Emily Dickinson," Allen Tate argues that the best poetry is written when a cultural tradition is coming to an end. When the once rigid forms of custom and ritual become increasingly flexible and porous, that is the time, according to Tate, to look for the emergence of a great writer. The poet can then toy with cultural forms, question them, look at them askance. Tate explains Dickinson's greatness by her autumnal, or wintry, feel for the traditions of American Puritanism. There is much of the Puritan in Dickinson's poems—her harsh moralism, her insistence on a personal and imperiled tie to God, her austerity of phrase. But the seedbed of a poet's soul, as Wordsworth called it, is ultimately unaccountable, and we have to look to deeper sources of memory and experience, even if many of these places are closed to us.

Proust made a distinction between two kinds of memory, voluntary and involuntary. Voluntary memory, built up by the patient retrieval of documents—the testimony of birth certificates, report cards, newspaper articles, letters—is quite vast for parts of Dickinson's life, though what we can retrieve from her childhood is scanty. Richard Sewall suggests this is because good children make bad biography; only misbehavior is recorded.

*Prose fragment, written on both sides of a
chiropodist's advertisement; text at right.*

Nor do her poems tell us much about her childhood. Dickinson's poetry is not a poetry of retrieval, as Wordsworth's often is. She is rarely autobiographical. But late in her life she wrote an insightful paragraph on a scrap of paper (a chiropodists's advertisement), and put it in her drawer:

> Two things I have lost with Childhood—the rapture of losing my shoe in the Mud and going Home barefoot, wading for Cardinal flowers and the mothers reproof which was more for my sake than her weary own for she frowned with a smile—now Mother and Cardinal flower are parts of a closed world—But is that all I have lost—memory drapes her lips.

The passage has the intensity of involuntary memory—which alone, according to Proust, gives us access to our own pasts. The mud, the shoe, and the flower (not just any flower but the cardinal flower, with its clusters of scarlet blossoms) have the luminous specificity, the sheer *there*-ness, of experience. It is as though we are suddenly admitted for a moment to the inside of her life.

What Dickinson has lost, as shown in this passage, is itself an experience of losing, as though even the facts—the shoe stuck in the mud—are evanescent. ("But are not all Facts Dreams as soon as we put them behind us?" she jotted on a piece of paper at about the same time.) She is more lucid than some of her biographers about the retrieval of the "parts of a closed world." On the other side of the piece of paper she wrote a sentence about our compensation for loss: "Did we not find as we lost we should make but a threadbare exhibition after a few years."

In nineteenth-century American letters there is an enduring anxiety about education. From Emerson's "The American Scholar" to *The Education of Henry Adams* writers brooded over what an American ought to learn. When Thomas Wentworth Higginson asked Dickinson about her background she answered, "I went to school—but in your manner of phrase—had no education." But she had a good liberal training with a strong scientific bent, as well as that intimacy with the Bible, the hymnal, and Shakespeare that literate churchgoing people in New England had.

Emily Dickinson resembles other writers who claimed that a sophisticated and thoughtful nearness to nature was as important as books. ("Books are for the scholar's idle times," Emerson proclaimed.) She wrote:

> To see the Summer Sky
> Is Poetry, though never in a Book it lie—
> True Poems flee—

If hers was a family committed to education it was also, especially in her generation (raised on Wordsworth and William Cullen Bryant), a family deeply involved with the natural world. Austin Dickinson, often troubled in his social relations, his career, and his marriage, found peace in nature. "He was perhaps the first," according to Polly Longsworth, who has devoted a good deal of study to his life, "to stand apart and look at the Amherst landscape with which he lived intimately, to appreciate, and also to improve." And he is remembered for his affair with Mabel Loomis Todd, the wife of the local astronomy professor. What brought them together was, among other things, their shared love for the outdoors.

In the late 1800s the arts and sciences did not seem as far apart as they have come to seem in our time. Mabel Todd, who once wrote to Austin that she was "thrilled with every bit of lichen on an old stone wall," was known for the beauty and accuracy of her nature paintings. Her study of the monarch butterfly was

Mabel Loomis Todd sent a sketch of Indian Pipes to ED in 1882 (p. 67), which was used on the cover of the first selection of Dickinson's poems (1890).

used for the frontispiece of *Butterflies of the Eastern United States and Canada*, by Samuel Scudder, the famous entomologist.

Looming behind Dickinson's education, and behind Austin's as well, is the figure of Edward Hitchcock, a leading botanist and geologist who was president of Amherst College from 1845 to 1854, and a major presence at the Academy, where Dickinson probably heard him lecture. He is an important instigator of the kind of intense, disciplined contemplation of nature one finds in Thoreau—who wrote an enthusiastic review of one of his books on plants. For Hitchcock the wonders of nature were the best proof of the workings of the divine in *this* world. Dickinson wrote to Higginson (who was himself the author of numerous nature essays): "When Flowers annually died and I was a child, I used to read Dr. Hitchcock's Book on the Flowers of North America. This comforted their Absence—assuring me they lived."

Dickinson's familiarity with the natural sciences is evident in many of her poems. She surprises her reader with words and metaphors culled from the modern science of her time, in contrast with the often explicitly anti-scientific poets of today. Sometimes she seems merely whimsical, as when she notes that "Science is very near us—I found a megatherium on my strawberry." We learn from the dictionary that a megatherium is a large extinct ground sloth. But more often she plunders science for apt analogies. Here is her witty version (as Richard Sewall points out) of the conservation of matter as proof of immortality:

> The Chemical conviction
> That Nought be lost
> Enable in Disaster
> My fractured Trust—
>
> The Faces of the Atoms
> If I shall see
> How more the Finished Creatures
> Departed me!

Her poems sometimes take on the tone of a scientist:

I think that the Root of the Wind is Water—
It would not sound so deep
Were it a Firmamental Product—
Airs no Oceans keep—
Mediterranean intonations—
To a Current's Ear—
There is a maritime conviction
In the Atmosphere—

or "After all Birds have been investigated and laid aside—
Nature imparts the little Blue-Bird." Her friend Samuel Bowles
was surprised at the lines in her poem about the snake, "He likes
a Boggy Acre —A Floor too cool for Corn."   Bowles, who
published the poem in the *Springfield Republican*, is supposed to
have asked, "How did that girl know that a boggy field wasn't
good for corn?"

   But her poems also reveal a recurring sense of surprise that the
world is put together the way it is. "How much can come/And
much can go,/And yet abide the World!" Sometimes she is content simply to list her observations:

"Nature" is what we see—
The Hill—the Afternoon—
Squirrel—Eclipse—the Bumble bee—

At other times she offers recipes to explain how the world is
composed:

To make a prairie it takes a clover and one bee,
One clover, and a bee,
And revery.
The revery alone will do,
If bees are few.

43

But her finest work pursues a deeper line of questioning, as though she were asking, with Thoreau, "Why do precisely these objects which we behold make a world?"

> Four Trees—upon a solitary Acre —
> Without Design
> Or Order, or Apparent Action—
> Maintain—
>
> The Sun—upon a Morning meets them—
> The Wind—
> No nearer Neighbor—have they—
> But God—
>
> The Acre gives them—Place —
> They—Him—Attention of Passer by—
> Of Shadow, or of Squirrel, haply—
> Or Boy—
>
> What Deed is Theirs unto the General Nature—
> What Plan
> They severally—retard—or further—
> Unknown—

This poem is usually read as though it asserted the random arrangement of the landscape, but it can be seen as far more positive in its awareness of an order that is "maintained," though it eludes our knowledge. What is more, this coherence depends on us, for it requires our "attention." So we must have eyes to see: "Not 'Revelation'—'tis—that waits,/But our unfurnished eyes."

· · ·

The crucial years for Dickinson as a poet are roughly from 1858 to 1864. Sometime in the late fifties she began to sew packets (or "fascicles") of poems together, as though for safekeeping. Lately there has been a good deal of argument, still inconclusive, about whether the packets constitute poetic sequences. Despite some speculation to the contrary, it seems that when she showed poems to her friends, they were not so arranged. Early in this period she found her own poetic voice, settling once and for all into simple ballad or hymn stanzas. She also gradually began to withdraw from society, until she saw few visitors and rarely left the house. "I do not cross my Father's ground to any House or town." It has escaped no one's notice that these were crucial years for the country as well.

Was it mere coincidence that Dickinson wrote most copiously during the years of the American Civil War? She gives us few clues. Scattered remarks in her letters suggest that the war seemed, mostly, far away: "War feels to me an oblique place." Austin paid for a replacement in the army, so her family was not directly involved. When Amherst boys died she sent letters and poems of condolence, what she called "the balsam word." She came to think of poetry as therapeutic, but wrote nothing that directly expressed her views on the war. She seems to refute Hawthorne's claim that "There is no remoteness of life and thought, no hermetically sealed seclusion, except, possibly, that of the grave, into which the disturbing influences of this war do not penetrate." He added, with a hint of irony, "I magnanimously considered that there is a kind of treason in insulating one's self from the universal fear and sorrow, and thinking one's idle thoughts in the dread time of civil war." Dickinson has been accused of such indifference.

"Mozart never commented on the political upheaval of the French Revolution," writes his latest biographer. "His response to the spirit of the age was *Figaro*." For a long time critics have looked for Dickinson's "Figaro." As early as 1931, Lewis Mumford wrote that "In Emily Dickinson's poems, even more than in Ambrose Bierce's stories of the war, even more than in Whitman's *Drum Taps*, was the marrow of American experience during the Civil War"—but he didn't identify which poems he meant. Most recently, the critic Shira Wolosky has claimed that the war is somehow the key to Dickinson's poetry. "Far from remaining detached from the civil conflagration, Dickinson internalized it," she argues in *Emily Dickinson: A Voice of War* (1985). Wolosky, citing Dickinson's frequent use of martial imagery, finds the Civil War lurking behind far more poems than those that have been linked, by letters and dates, to specific battles and Amherst casualties. (R.P. Blackmur, writing in 1937, made the same point.) But like many of Dickinson's critics, Wolosky is quite literal in her marshaling of the evidence. Consider the following:

> Whole Gulfs—of Red, and Fleets—of Red—
> And Crews—of solid Blood—
> Did place about the West—Tonight—
> As 'twere specific Ground—

Wolosky detects here "a traumatized view of sunset," in which "Dickinson perceives the day's decline" as "terrible and fearful." But the wit of the poem outweighs (or rather lightens) its trauma; the battle is merely a clever conceit for the sunset. In addition, Wolosky has to parry the presence of martial imagery in Dickinson's poems *before* 1861: "The rhetoric of war and the conflict of issues were already making themselves felt in the national consciousness." Perhaps. But the rhetoric of war had also sounded in Shakespeare and Byron and Emily Brontë—writers Dickinson loved.

The idea that Dickinson was particularly prolific during this

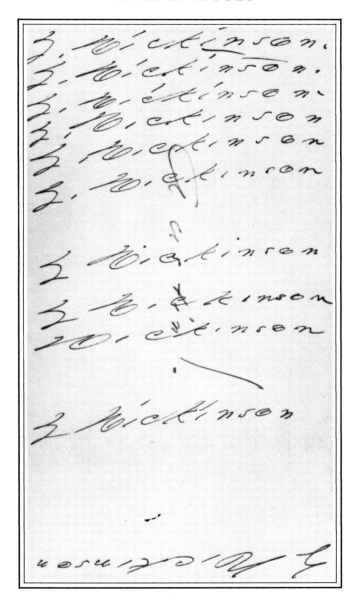

A page of signatures, on an envelope inscribed "Austin."

Thomas Wentworth Higginson, with his daughter.

period has great appeal for critics. Alfred Kazin writes (in 1984): "The Civil War is not named, although in 1862–63 it led to her writing more than a poem a day—and some of her fiercest poems." That is, if you divide by 365. But one has to be suspicious of this (very widespread) poem-a-day notion. We don't know how or when she wrote. Maybe she wrote poetry only on Sundays (seven poems a week), or recopied poems written in the 1850s and disposed of the originals. In any case the dating of most of the poems is approximate at best, based mainly on changes in her handwriting. The fact is, critics want to believe that the war affected Dickinson's writing—"*it led* to her writing more than a poem a day." This view makes her seem less reclusive, more responsible, more an American writer, but there is little evidence to support it.

None of this means that Dickinson was politically irresponsible, but we are unfair to our artists when we demand explicit political commentary from them. If they acquiesce, the result is often bland and forgettable. They are on surer footing when they follow their own imaginative promptings. As Dickinson herself remarked, "I never try to lift the words which I cannot hold." If she says little about the Civil War, we cannot conclude that it was unimportant to her.

A likelier theory is that the Civil War coincided with Dickinson's coming of age as a writer. She was in her early thirties, eager to be recognized as a poet, and had found a form and diction she was anxious to explore. In 1862 she first wrote to Thomas Wentworth Higginson, man of letters, who had just published a piece in the *Atlantic* called "Letter to a Young Contributor." In his essay Higginson encouraged unpublished writers to seek an audience for their work. That he was also identified with many public causes, including Abolition and the rights of women, that he was involved in the John Brown conspiracy, that he was soon, as Colonel Higginson, to lead a black regiment in the war, seems to have meant little to Dickinson. She wanted an audience for her poems, and he was a public figure who had expressed interest in young, unknown writers.

Higginson was not the only person Dickinson approached for advice about her work, but one feels awkward discussing her "literary circle." Her biographer Richard Sewall has shown that she was not as isolated as had been assumed. She had literary friends and correspondents, among them some of the leading editors, journalists, and writers in New England; and yet one cannot help feeling disappointed at their lack of perception. Couldn't they see that a genius was living and writing in their midst? But as Emerson observes, "There is somewhat touching in the madness with which the passing age mischooses the object on which all candles shine, and all eyes are turned." Emily Dickinson, the lawyer's daughter, judge of the Indian bread competition at the Amherst Cattle Show, a great poet? As she herself paraphrased the Bible: "the prophet had no fame in his immediate Town."

Higginson, who had some perspective, thought "Amherst must be a *nest* of poetesses." To his credit, he found Dickinson unusual, but perhaps too much so to be published; he preferred the easier melodies of another Amherst poetess (and childhood friend of Emily Dickinson), Helen Hunt Jackson, author of the popular novel, *Ramona*. Higginson visited Dickinson twice in the early 1870s and reported to his wife: "I never was with any one who drained my nerve power so much. Without touching her, she drew from me. I am glad not to live near her. She often thought me tired. . . ." If only, we wonder, Dickinson had come to the attention of Emerson (who lectured in Amherst and stayed at her brother's house), or Whitman, or Thoreau—someone who could discount her eccentricity and appreciate her genius. But she chose Higginson as her guide—Higginson who

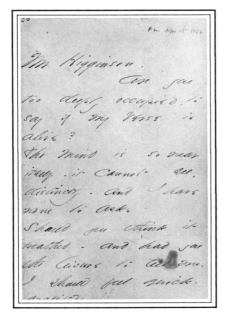

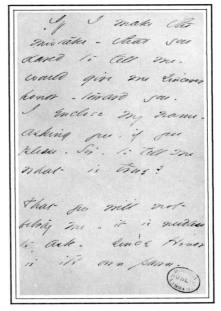

Dickinson's first letter to Higginson,
April 15, 1862, enclosing four poems.

"Mr. Higginson.

Are you too deeply occupied to say if
my Verse is alive?
The Mind is so near itself—it cannot
see, distinctly—and I have none to
ask—
Should you think it breathed—and
had you the leisure to tell me, I
should feel quick gratitude—

If I make the mistake—that you dared to tell me—would give me sincerer honor
—toward you—
I enclose my name—asking you, if you please—Sir—to tell me what is true?
That you will not betray me—it is needless to ask—since Honor is its own
pawn—

once remarked: "It is no discredit to Walt Whitman that he wrote 'Leaves of Grass,' only that he did not burn it afterwards."

Susan Gilbert, who married Austin Dickinson in 1856, was Dickinson's first critic, and her encouragement, while often rather obtuse, probably helped Dickinson continue writing in the fifties. But it was to male mentors that Dickinson increasingly turned for confirmation—probably because they controlled the literary press and the rest of the machinery of fame. There is something highly theatrical in these relationships. It is as though Dickinson wanted to play Heloise—the identity of her Abelard was not particularly important. Dickinson liked to call her mentors "master" or "preceptor." After she died three extraordinary letters were found in her papers. They are passionate love letters, very "literary," and heavily redacted. We don't know whether they were ever sent or whether they were even addressed to anyone in particular. They may well have been literary and emotional exercises—like the letters Charlotte Brontë addressed in French to her Belgian "master," Constantin Heger. But literary sleuths love a mystery, and for a hundred years the identity of the master has been a favorite guessing game.

Biographical speculation about a possible romance, the failure of which led to her withdrawal, focused for many years on Charles Wadsworth, a famous minister whom Dickinson probably met in Philadelphia in 1855, on the same excursion that took her to Washington to visit her father in Congress. Source-hunters have found many parallels in passages from Wadsworth's sermons and Dickinson's poems. Such parallels may, however, simply show how homogeneous and conventional religious rhetoric was in America in the middle of the nineteenth century. In 1862 Wadsworth left Philadelphia for a church in San Francisco, thereby (according to melodramatic speculation) breaking Dickinson's heart. Mark Twain heard

Wadsworth preach in California and was impressed by his sense of humor:

> Dr. Wadsworth never fails to preach an able sermon; but every now and then, with an admirable assumption of not being aware of it, he will get off a first rate joke and then frown severely at any one who is surprised into smiling at it. . . . Several people there on Sunday suddenly laughed and as suddenly stopped again, when he gravely gave the Sunday school books a blast and spoke of "the good little boys in them who always went to Heaven, and the bad little boys who infallibly got drowned on Sunday," and then swept a savage frown around the house and blighted every smile in the congregation.

Late in her life Dickinson made some sentimental remarks about her friendship with Wadsworth, but their relations, thinly documented and thickly embroidered, may well have meant more to her in retrospect than in the 1850s.

More recently Samuel Bowles, editor of the *Springfield Republican* and close friend of Austin and Emily Dickinson, has become a leading suspect. Sewall leans in his favor and the critic Karl Keller leans overboard: "In her letters and poems to Bowles (and these most certainly include the three Master letters of 1858–61). . . ." Bowles was energetic, sexy, and smart, and he seems to have taken a no-nonsense approach to Dickinson that she found disarming and exciting. An often repeated anecdote, that may or may not be true, concerns a visit Bowles payed to the Homestead sometime around 1877. Dickinson apparently refused to come down the stairs to see him, so he shouted: "Emily, you damned rascal! No more of this nonsense! I've traveled all the way from Springfield to see you. Come down at once." Rumor has it she came down, and was never more witty.

In the last years of her life Dickinson fell in love with Otis Lord, a distinguished judge on the Massachusetts Supreme Court. He returned her love and may have proposed marriage. Certain of her letters suggest she turned him down, though we don't know why. "Don't you know you are happiest while I withhold and not confer—" she wrote him. "Don't you know that 'No' is the wildest word we consign to language?" Perhaps it would have been more surprising if she'd married him. She had lived fifty years at home and a move would have been extraordinarily disruptive. This last (and perhaps first) romance is a satisfying, autumnal image with which to leave Dickinson's life. It is jarring, however, to learn that the judge's niece and housekeeper, Abbie Farley, annoyed by his attentions to Emily Dickinson, called her a "little hussy. . . . Loose morals. She was crazy about men. Even tried to get Judge Lord. Insane, too."

What all these masters, mentors, and preceptors did for Dickinson's writing is difficult to say. Probably not much. Most of them—Susan Gilbert, Higginson, Bowles—offered her obtuse directions on how to improve the poems. But she seems to have survived their advice—the "surgery" she thanked Higginson for—by ignoring it. Her documented relations with important literary figures in New England make her seem, ultimately, even lonelier than she had seemed according to popular legend.

While most poets spin a web of literary affiliations, which in turn helps readers place them, Emily Dickinson's web is scarcely visible. We have little sense of what she read or of what she thought of it. She was aware of the ongoing debate about the emergence of a national literature. She probably had read Emerson's "American Scholar" or knew its arguments, and we know she read Higginson's "Plea for Culture." And yet she seems remarkably uninterested in her American contemporaries. She has nothing much to say about Emerson. When he visited Amherst in 1857, and stayed at Austin's house next door, she commented that he looked "as if he had come from where dreams are born." When Higginson gave her his own *Short Studies of American Authors*, she offered a few opinions: "Of Poe, I know too little to think—Hawthorne appalls, entices—Mrs. Helen Hunt Jackson soars to your estimate lawfully as a Bird, but of Howells and James, one hesitates." Her most famous remark on an American writer is about Whitman: "I never read his Book—but was told it was disgraceful." None of this is particularly striking, although that in itself is interesting. In her book *Literary Women* Ellen Moers observes, with some justice, "The real hidden scandal of Emily Dickinson's life is . . . her embarrassing ignorance of American literature."

Of course Moers is only half serious. And one reason Dickinson may have withheld from Higginson what she thought of American literature was that she knew he wouldn't be particularly appreciative. She played the role of his pupil. She was always telling him how small she was, thus implying how big he was. Her opinions about those great American writers could hardly matter. But it is significant that her opinion of Helen Hunt Jackson's poetry outweighs the others. Dickinson was extraordinarily interested in literature by women; she admired the Brontës, George Eliot ("'What do I think of *Middlemarch*?' What do I think of glory—"), and, above all, Elizabeth Barrett Browning. What Dickinson loved in Barrett Browning was probably, as Moers suggests, "her confident use of female experience and female accessories—the clothes, the looks, the domestic chores of a woman—for universal purposes." Barrett Browning, by writing of ordinary women's experience in *Aurora Leigh*, seems to have opened up to Dickinson the validity of her own existence. In some of her finest love poems Dickinson uses details from her daily life to anchor her passion:

> If you were coming in the Fall,
> I'd brush the Summer by
> With half a smile, and half a spurn,
> As Housewives do, a Fly.

> If I could see you in a year,
> I'd wind the months in balls—
> And put them each in separate Drawers,
> For fear the numbers fuse—

> .   .   .

> But, now, uncertain of the length
> Of this, that is between,
> It goads me, like the Goblin Bee—
> That will not state—its sting.

Dickinson wrote three poems about Elizabeth Barrett Browning, all expressing her gratitude. One begins "I went to thank her." Another describes the experience of first reading "that Foreign Lady" as a "Conversion of the Mind."

> I think I was enchanted
> When first a sombre Girl—
> I read that Foreign Lady—
> The Dark—felt beautiful—

> .   .   .

The Bees—became as Butterflies—
The Butterflies—as Swans—
Approached—and spurned the narrow Grass—
And just the meanest Tunes

That Nature murmured to herself
To keep herself in Cheer—
I took for Giants—practising
Titanic Opera—

The Days—to Mighty Metres stept—
The Homeliest—adorned
As if unto a Jubilee
'Twere suddenly confirmed—

Reading the English poet thus gave Dickinson what was already her own, even what was "meanest" and "homeliest."

If the major task of literary historians in the decades after Dickinson's death was to try (often without much luck) to relate her to American Puritanism, and to place her in relation to such distinguished older writers as Emerson, Hawthorne, and Melville, it has been the aim of much recent criticism to regard her in light of another inheritance, her explicit debt to women writers.

But poets echo and allude to earlier poets in subtler ways. Conrad Aiken, introducing a selection of Dickinson's poems for British readers in 1924, barked, "The meagreness of literary allusion is astounding." While much more has been deciphered recently, the references are often to second-rate stuff—lines from Higginson's essays, stray bits of popular romances— hardly *literary* allusion at all. But the meagreness was probably deliberate. Consider a remark Dickinson made in a letter to Higginson:

I marked a line in One Verse—because I met it after I made it—and never consciously touch a paint, mixed by another person.

This may help explain why she held so resolutely to her simple hymn or ballad measures, almost never venturing into the grander rhythms of iambic pentameter. It may well have seemed to her like "a paint mixed by another person"—by Shakespeare or Milton or Keats.

If a subtle sexism has focused our attention on the men in Dickinson's life, it has also diverted our attention from the philosophical sophistication of her poems; we are perhaps unaccustomed to look to women as great thinkers. But Dickinson's meditations were as deep and complex and as accurately expressed as Emerson's or Thoreau's. She was diffident about this, and told Higginson, "When I try to organize—my little Force explodes—and leaves me bare and charred—." But thinking was apparently a daily discipline for her. She reportedly asked Higginson: "How do most people live without any thoughts. There are many people in the world (you must have noticed them in the street) How do they live. How do they get strength to put on their clothes in the morning?" Higginson was shocked at this undemocratic attitude. But what it suggests is how vital the life of the mind was to her.

> A Thought went up my mind today—
> That I have had before—
> But did not finish—some way back—
> I could not fix the Year—

Nor where it went—nor why it came
The second time to me—
Nor definitely, what it was—
Have I the Art to say—

But somewhere—in my Soul—I know—
I've met the Thing before—
It just reminded me—'twas all—
And came my way no more—

This is an entry in a sort of diary of the mind's activities.

"We shall never learn where she got the rich quality of her mind," Allen Tate remarks; but there are several places where one can look for clues, beginning with the daily discipline of writing letters. Today, when letter writing has disappeared, or is practiced as a faded art, it is hard to conceive of the importance of private letters in the nineteenth century, especially among literate women. When Dickinson wrote in 1885, "A letter is a joy of Earth—/It is denied the Gods," she meant that the Gods are unlucky not to have the pleasure of receiving letters; she also meant there's no mail from heaven. She carried on many correspondences. Some were destroyed, some lost. But more than a thousand of her letters are gathered in the three volumes published in 1958. These extraordinary letters show, among other things, how seriously Dickinson, her siblings, and her adult friends took the art of letter writing. It was an art that was learned, with rules and forms, and practiced constantly. Henry James described New England as "a society in which introspection, thanks to the want of other entertainment, played almost the part of a social resource." The solitary discipline of letter writing, as practiced by Dickinson, gives us a sense of the rhetoric and order of this rich inner speech.

The reading of letters requires the same emphatic solitude, as the following poem suggests. It is also about reading poems—picking their locks to find their meanings:

> The Way I read a Letter's—this—
> 'Tis first—I lock the Door—
> And push it with my fingers—next—
> For transport it be sure—
>
> And then I go the furthest off
> To counteract a knock—
> Then draw my little Letter forth
> And slowly pick the lock—
>
> Then—glancing narrow, at the Wall—
> And narrow at the floor
> For firm Conviction of a Mouse
> Not exorcised before—
>
> Peruse how infinite I am
> To no one that You—know—
> And sigh for lack of Heaven—but not
> The Heaven God bestow—

The guided reflection of prayer, together with the private letter, is Dickinson's favorite analogue for poetry.

> Prayer is the little implement
> Through which Men reach
> Where Presence—is denied them.
> They fling their Speech
>
> By means of it—in God's Ear—

The legacy of Puritanism, with its stress on the individual person's relation with God, and the constant self-inspection this requires, has often been noted as an influence on Dickinson's poetry.

The place of memory in her poetry has not received enough attention. I suspect Dickinson knew all her own poetry by heart, as well as huge passages from Shakespeare, Milton, the Bible, Elizabeth Barrett Browning; she often quotes from these in her letters. She writes of memory as a large interior structure—

> Remembrance has a Rear and Front—
> 'Tis something like a House—
> It has a Garret also
> For Refuse and the Mouse.

—in which she can file away her experience, her reading, and her thinking. Memory is also, with its mechanisms for repression, the source of the Gothic horror she is so fond of. See, for example, the poem that begins "I years had been from home," as well as the poem above, which concludes:

> Besides the deepest Cellar
> That ever Mason laid—
> Look to it by its Fathoms
> Ourselves be not pursued—

The disciplined observation of nature one finds in such writers as Hitchcock, Thoreau, and Higginson also contributed to the "rich quality of her mind." These writers helped key up the contemplation of the natural world until it became almost a spiritual exercise. We know these writings were particularly vital to Dickinson. The seasons were her rosary.

It is common to lump together many of Dickinson's poems as

"nature poetry," but these poems are of several different kinds. Dickinson rarely observes nature with "objective" or deadening detachment. Nature for her is vital, but one can distinguish two ways in which she portrays it, which might be called *animation* and *animism*. The first produces a particular kind of allegory of human life. Dickinson employs a cast of little characters—bees, flowers, birds—to perform human pleasures and predicaments:

> A Bee his burnished Carriage
> Drove boldly to a Rose—
> Combinedly alighting—
> Himself—his Carriage was—
> The Rose received his visit
> With frank tranquillity
> Withholding not a Crescent
> To his Cupidity—

This elegant and mild eroticism reaches the level of great art in her poem "Wild Nights." She has many poems in a similar cartoon-like mode ("The Rat is the Concisest Tenant./He pays no Rent") and other characters, such as God and Death and Eternity, can make an appearance. This is a variety of "grotesque," as the critic Barton St. Armand observes, that has little to do with nature or landscape.

The second kind of nature poem attributes to nature and to the landscape a life of its own. Ruskin, one of Dickinson's favorite writers, gave this tendency a name: "All violent feelings," he wrote, "produce in us a falseness in all our impressions of external things, which I would generally characterize as the 'pathetic fallacy.'" We easily forget that Ruskin did not consider this illusion necessarily a fault. On the contrary, he believed it was used by some of the finest poets—Keats, Coleridge, Tennyson.

Only the very finest, Shakespeare and Dante and Homer, managed to rise above their passion. Some of Dickinson's poems use this device in an automatic way that hardly seems pathetic at all, since no strong feeling is involved.

> The Wind begun to rock the Grass
> With threatening Tunes and low—
> He threw a Menace at the Earth—
> A Menace at the Sky.
>
> The Leaves unhooked themselves from Trees—
> And started all abroad
> The Dust did scoop itself like Hands
> And threw away the Road.

As the imagery develops—"The Lightning showed a Yellow Beak/And then a livid Claw"—the poem seems increasingly a cartoon-like portrayal of a storm.

But in her best poems about landscape, Dickinson senses the truth in pathetic fallacy, that nature is a world of life rather than of death.

> Further in Summer than the Birds
> Pathetic from the Grass
> A minor Nation celebrates
> Its unobtrusive Mass.
>
> No Ordinance be seen
> So gradual the Grace
> A pensive Custom it becomes
> Enlarging Loneliness.

Antiquest felt at Noon
When August burning low
Arise this spectral Canticle
Repose to typify

Remit as yet no Grace
No Furrow on the Glow
Yet a Druidic Difference
Enhances Nature now

It is one of Dickinson's most beautiful poems. The same music of insects can be heard in Keats's "To Autumn" and in Wallace Stevens's "Sunday Morning."

If Ruskin complains that poets sometimes see life where there isn't any, Dickinson's boast is that poets bring things to life.

I reckon—when I count at all—
First—Poets—Then the Sun—
Then Summer—Then the Heaven of God—
And then—the List is done—

But, looking back—the First so seems
To Comprehend the Whole—
The Others look a needless Show—
So I write—Poets—All—

Their Summer—lasts a Solid Year—
They can afford a Sun
The East—would deem extravagant—
And if the Further Heaven—

Be Beautiful as they prepare
For Those who worship Them—
It is too difficult a Grace—
To justify the Dream—

Dickinson is never complacent about the poet's vocation, however. She felt hemmed in by mysteries and learned to live with them. "In a life that stopped guessing," she told Susan Gilbert, "you and I should not feel at home." She loved the way the ancient literary genre of the riddle registers this sense of uncertainty—about nature, life, and death. Some of her most popular poems, especially with children, have such obvious "answers" that the subjects might as well be specified.

I like to see it lap the Miles—
And lick the Valleys up—
And stop to feed itself at Tanks—
And then—prodigious step

Around a Pile of Mountains—
And supercilious peer
In Shanties—by the sides of Roads—
And then a Quarry pare

To fit its Ribs
And crawl between
Complaining all the while
In horrid—hooting stanza—
Then chase itself down Hill—

And neigh like Boanerges—
Then— punctual as a Star
Stop—docile and omnipotent
At its own stable door—

This expands the familiar metaphor of the "iron horse." Dickinson also wrote playful riddles in prose, like this one in a letter to her nephew Ned on his third birthday: "Emily knows a Man who drives a Coach like a Thimble, and turns the Wheel all day with his Heel—His name is Bumblebee."

She was proud of the wit and charm of such poems. When Mabel Loomis Todd sent her a drawing in 1882, she responded, "I cannot make an Indian Pipe but please accept a Humming Bird," thus giving away the answer of the poem she enclosed:

> A Route of Evanescence
> With a revolving Wheel—
> A Resonance of Emerald—
> A Rush of Cochineal—
> And every Blossom on the Bush
> Adjusts its tumbled Head—
> The mail from Tunis, probably,
> An easy Morning's Ride—

The poem catches the sheer oddity of the hummingbird, a fitting exchange for the weird white flowers and stalks of the Indian Pipes. In poems like this "the subject is not described but circumscribed: a circle of words drawn around it," as Northrop Frye has aptly written of literary riddles in general.

If the riddle asks readers to guess what something is, another literary form, the definition, tells them. Dickinson, who said that for several years her lexicon was her only companion, framed definitions that can't be found in any dictionary. These are often darker than her riddles, as though she is seeking words for things that elude them. "Doom is the House without the Door," she writes, or "Faith—is the Pierless Bridge/Supporting what We see/Unto the Scene that We do not—."Has the in-

An exchange of gifts. Mabel Todd sent to ED a drawing of Indian Pipes, on black gilt-edge panel, on September 24, 1882.

ED responded: "Dear friend, I cannot make an Indian Pipe but please accept a Humming Bird."

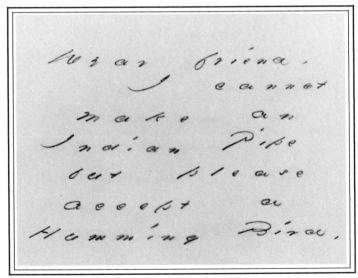

somniac's hell been better described than in this definition
poem?

> Remorse—is Memory—awake—
> Her Parties all astir—
> A Presence of Departed Acts—
> At window—and at Door—
>
> Its Past—set down before the Soul
> And lighted with a Match—
> Perusal—to facilitate—
> And help Belief to stretch—
>
> Remorse is cureless—the Disease
> Not even God—can heal—
> For 'tis His institution—and
> The Adequate of Hell—

Death is the ultimate mystery for Dickinson; no matter how
wise we are, "through a riddle at the last,/Sagacity must go."
She can try to ward off the horror with a glib definition: "Death
is the supple Suitor/That wins at last," whose "stealthy Wooing"
is pursued by "pallid innuendoes." Even when she is wondering
about the resurrection she can be witty and playful:

> Some things that fly there be—
> Birds—Hours—the Bumblebee—
> Of these no Elegy.
>
> Some things that stay there be—
> Grief—Hills—Eternity—
> Nor this behooveth me.

There are that resting, rise.
Can I expound the skies?
How still the Riddle lies!

But in her best poems she is anxious about the boundaries of
what we know—"The Doubt like the Mosquito, buzzes round
my faith"—and uncertainty grows into a sense of religious
mystery.

It was not Death, for I stood up,
And all the Dead, lie down—
It was not Night, for all the Bells
Put out their Tongues, for Noon.

It was not Frost, for on my Flesh
I felt Siroccos—crawl—
Nor Fire—for just my Marble feet
Could keep a Chancel, cool—

And yet, it tasted, like them all,
The Figures I have seen
Set orderly, for Burial,
Reminded me, of mine—

As if my life were shaven,
And fitted to a frame,
And could not breathe without a key,
And 'twas like Midnight, some—

When everything that ticked—has stopped—
And Space stares all around—
Or Grisly frosts—first Autumn morns,
Repeal the Beating Ground—

But, most, like Chaos—Stopless—cool—
Without a Chance, or Spar—
Or even a Report of Land—
To justify—Despair.

Riddle and definition converge in this poem; we feel that the extremities of human experience have pushed words to their limit. "Had we the first intimation of the Definition of Life," Dickinson once told two of her young cousins, "the calmest of us would be Lunatics!"

And yet a remarkable sanity reigns over Dickinson's poetry, as though she has taken the measure of her life, and made the choices that satisfied her. If her poems are full of uncertainty so are our lives. "I shall know why—when Time is over—/and I have ceased to wonder why," she wrote. She herself seems to have enjoyed being a riddle to others, as Richard Sewall has remarked, and the mysteries of her life will continue to fascinate us. But the riddles of her poetry, however mystifying, are there to be read.

Reception

My life has been too simple and stern to embarrass any," Emily Dickinson once remarked, and it is difficult to imagine a life more completely given over to a single occupation—the writing of poetry. But the history of how her poetry has been received is bewilderingly complex. In the hundred years since her death Dickinson has been discovered, or recovered, several times by her critics. In a sense, a poet has as many lives as she has readers, but literary historians must distinguish the tendencies of whole generations of readers. To simplify, we may say that Dickinson has had at least three lives since her death, and these different Emily Dickinsons, far from supplanting one another, have survived into our own time.

Though Dickinson died in 1886, the 1890s was the crucial decade for the life of her poetry. Without the efforts of her family and friends we might not have retrieved the poems at all. Now, our impression of the 1890s has been radically changed by new information—generally known only since 1974—about Austin Dickinson's passionate affair with Mabel Loomis Todd. Not only did the lovers correspond in letters that they preserved, but Mabel kept an elaborate diary in which she recorded in minute detail her own erotic and emotional calendar. She took an extraordinary interest in the most intimate aspects of her life, and historians of nineteenth-century sexuality are grateful. The affair apparently had Emily Dickinson's approval. She was partic-

Lavinia Dickinson in 1896.

ularly close to Austin, and probably knew that her sister-in-law found sex and childbearing repugnant. She certainly knew the marriage was not happy, and she may have felt that her brother deserved something better.

Lavinia Dickinson was amazed, after her sister's death, to find hundreds of poems and fragments—some in fair copies, some in drafts, some scribbled on scraps of paper—crammed into the drawer of Emily's bureau. Lavinia took the poems to Susan Gilbert, Austin's wife, expecting help in getting them published, but Sue was evidently not enthusiastic. Lavinia then appealed to Mabel to undertake the task of selecting and editing the poems. Mabel had no doubt about their value, and she persuaded Thomas Wentworth Higginson to help bring out a selection. But after three slim volumes appeared, entitled *Poems* (first, second, and third series—published in 1890, 1891, and 1896), Lavinia and Mabel quarreled over a piece of land that Austin, who died in 1895, had left to his mistress. The remaining poems were boxed again, in a locked chest, where they remained for almost forty years, until Mabel's daughter, Millicent Todd Bingham, made them public.

Mabel Loomis Todd was an extremely talented woman—praised for her physical beauty, her fine voice, her paintings. Hearing her recite Dickinson's poems evidently did much to persuade Higginson of their worth, and she lectured widely to publicize the poetry. But she hasn't been credited enough (though Sewall made a start) for her abilities as a literary critic. She remarked, in the preface to the second series of *Poems*:

> Like impressionist pictures, or Wagner's rugged music, the very absence of conventional form challenges attention. In Emily Dickinson's exacting hands, the especial, intrinsic fitness of a particular order of words might not be sacrificed to anything virtually extrinsic; and her verses all show a strange cadence of inner rhythmical music. Lines are always daringly constructed, and the "thought-rhyme" appears frequently,—appealing, indeed, to an unrecognized sense more elusive than hearing.

Her comments stand up well against more recent criticism. Todd had a sense of the importance in Dickinson's poetry of what T. S. Eliot called the "auditory imagination," the "strange cadence of inner rhythmical music" Todd detected in the verse. Consider for example the compelling first line, "Further in

Summer than the Birds," in the rich assonance of which the critic David Porter hears the murmur of insects.

It has been suggested that a major reason for the success of *Poems* (1890) was a fin-de-siècle nostalgia for old New England. The legend of Emily Dickinson as a charming, unschooled eccentric from an out-of-the-way New England town already had currency in the 1890s. Though this image certainly had a role in the reception of her work, it would appear that Dickinson seemed, even to the audiences of the 1890s, more revolutionary than reactionary; Todd's comparison of her poems to Wagner and Impressionism reveals that Dickinson seemed avant-garde. She was labeled early as the "last flower of New England Puritanism"—the flower metaphor became a commonplace in later criticism, but William Dean Howells, perhaps the most successful and influential novelist, editor, and critic of the 1880s and 90s, while recognizing her roots in New England culture, also compared her to the German poet and wit Heinrich Heine —who used similar meters and stanzas—and to Blake. In the long essay Howells devoted to Dickinson, published in *Harper's* in 1891, he writes:

> Colonel Higginson speaks of her "curious indifference to all conventional rules of verse," but he adds that "when a thought takes one's breath away, a lesson on grammar seems an impertinence." He notes "the quality suggestive of the poetry of William Blake" in her, but he leaves us the chance to say that it is Blake who had read Emerson who had read Blake. The fantasy is as often Blakian as the philosophy is Emersonian; but after feeling this again and again, one is ready to declare that the utterance of this most singular and authentic spirit would have been the same if there had never been an Emerson or a Blake in the world. . . .

Here is something that seems compact of both Emerson and Blake, with a touch of Heine too:

> I taste a liquor never brewed,
> From tankards scooped in pearl;
> Not all the vats upon the Rhine
> Yield such an alcohol!
>
> Inebriate of air am I,
> And debauchee of dew,
> Reeling, through endless summer days,
> From inns of molten blue.
>
> When landlords turn the drunken bee
> Out of the foxglove's door,
> When butterflies renounce their drams,
> I shall but drink the more!
>
> Till seraphs swing their snowy hats,
> And saints to windows run,
> To see the little tippler
> Leaning against the sun!

"The strange Poems of Emily Dickinson," he wrote, "we think will form something like an intrinsic experience with the understanding reader of them." For cultivated readers of the 1890s Dickinson seemed "the latest thing." Some English critics had dealt harshly with her ("'Alcohol' does not rhyme to pearl," wrote one, "she reminds us of no sane or educated writer"), and there was an element of national pride in the defense of a native poet. Alice James, the gifted sister of William and Henry James, read Dickinson's poems in 1892 and was pleased to find excellent poetry—excellent American poetry—that British readers had proved deaf to:

It is reassuring to hear the English pronouncement that Emily Dickinson is fifth-rate, they have such a capacity for missing quality; the robust evades them equally with the subtle. Her being sicklied o'er with T. W. Higginson makes one quake lest there be a latent flaw which escapes one's vision—but what tomes of philosophy *résumés* the cheap farce or expresses the highest point of view of the aspiring soul more completely than the following—

> How dreary to be somebody
> How public, like a frog
> To tell your name the livelong day
> To an admiring bog!

In a similar vein Howells stressed Dickinson's Americanness, and her specifically New England genius.

There is no hint of what turned her life in upon itself, and probably this was its natural evolution, or involution, from tendencies inherent in the New England, or the Puritan, spirit. . . .

"Such things could have come only from a woman's heart to which the experiences in a New England town have brought more knowledge of death than of life. Terribly unsparing many of these strange poems are, but true as the grave and certain as mortality. . . .

"All the Puritan longing for sincerity, for veracious conduct, which in some good New England women's natures is almost a hysterical shriek, makes its exultant grim assertion in these lines:

REAL

I like a look of agony,
Because I know it's true;
Men do not sham convulsion,
Nor simulate a throe.

The eyes glaze once, and that is death.
Impossible to feign
The beads upon the forehead
By homely anguish strung.

But Howells is also attentive to the deliberate artistry of the poems:

Few of the poems in the book are long, but none of the short, quick impulses of intense feeling or poignant thought can be called fragments. They are each a compassed whole, a sharply finished point, and there is evidence, circumstantial and direct, that the author spared no pains in the perfect expression of her ideals. Nothing, for example, could be added that would say more than she has said in four lines:

Presentiment is that long shadow on the lawn
Indicative that suns go down;
The notice to the startled grass
That darkness is about to pass.

Occasionally, the outside of the poem, so to speak, is left so rough, so rude, that the art seems to have faltered. But there is apparent to reflection the fact that the artist meant just this harsh exterior to remain, and that no grace of smoothness could have imparted her intention as it does. It is the soul of an abrupt, exalted New England woman that speaks in such brokenness.

He concludes with a fine tribute to Dickinson as an American artist:

> If nothing else had come out of our life but this strange poetry we should feel that in the work of Emily Dickinson, America, or New England rather, had made a distinctive addition to the literature of the world, and could not be left out of any record of it; and the interesting and important thing is that this poetry is as characteristic of our life as our business enterprise, our political turmoil, our demagogism, our millionairism. "Listen!" says Mr. James McNeill Whistler in that "Ten o'Clock" lecture of his which must have made his hearers feel very much lectured indeed, not to say browbeaten,—"Listen! There never was an artistic period. There never was an art-loving nation." But there were moments and there were persons to whom art was dear, and Emily Dickinson was one of these persons, one of these moments in a national life, and she could as well happen in Amherst, Mass., as in Athens, Att.

Though the *Poems* of 1890 sold well, Dickinson remained a subterranean taste from about 1897 to 1924. Barely mentioned in literary histories of the time and rarely included in anthologies, she had a brief success in 1914 with the publication of *The Single Hound* (mostly poems that Dickinson had sent to Susan Gilbert, edited by Sue's daughter, Martha Dickinson Bianchi). Reviewers noticed similarities between these poems and the current methods of the Imagists—that loosely convened school of poets, including Ezra Pound, H. D., and Amy Lowell—who wished to make a break with the traditions of American and

British poetry. They aimed for a new precision in their use of language, uncluttered with what was conventionally considered "poetic."

But it was in the 1920s and 30s that Dickinson really triumphed. Despite the continuing efforts of her niece, Mrs. Bianchi, to preserve the sentimental image of Dickinson as an eccentric spinster who was disappointed in love and wrote charming poems about birds and flowers, critics discerned a tougher and more sophisticated poet. She seemed less the vestige of an era, "the last flower of New England Puritanism," than the beginning of a new movement—an early rebel from the genteel conventions of Henry Wadsworth Longfellow and John Greenleaf Whittier, and a fit companion to Walt Whitman as an American iconoclast. Hart Crane, whose great poem "The Bridge" was a tribute to American heroism and vision, published a poem in 1927 that reflected this image of Dickinson.

TO EMILY DICKINSON

You who desired so much—in vain to ask—
Yet fed your hunger like an endless task,
Dared dignify the labor, bless the quest—
Achieved that stillness ultimately best,

Being, of all, least sought for: Emily, hear!
O sweet, dead Silencer, most suddenly clear
When singing that Eternity possessed
And plundered momently in every breast;

—Truly no flower yet withers in your hand,
The harvest you descried and understand
Needs more than wit to gather, love to bind.
Some reconcilement of remotest mind—

Leaves Ormus rubyless, and Ophir chill.
Else tears heap all within one clay-cold hill.

In 1924 Conrad Aiken edited a British volume of *Selected Poems of Emily Dickinson* with a preface that is the first of what are now recognized as the classic essays on Dickinson's poetry. The "New Critics" Allen Tate, R. P. Blackmur, and Yvor Winters also wrote important pieces on her work in the following years. We must keep in mind that these critics were reading Dickinson's poems in often heavily-edited versions. While praising Dickinson in a 1932 essay, Tate, a Southern poet and critic who was a friend of Crane, used a title that she never intended and a version of the poem that omits a stanza and changes some key words, especially in the third and fourth stanzas. But the essay is representative of the careful attention to language and technique that the "New Critics" devoted to Dickinson's work. (The poem, restored in 1955, is printed at right.)

One of the perfect poems in English is "The Chariot," and it illustrates better than anything else she wrote the special quality of her mind:

Because I could not stop for death,
He kindly stopped for me;
The carriage held but just ourselves
And immortality.

We slowly drove, he knew no haste,
And I had put away
My labor, and my leisure too,
For his civility.

We passed the school where children played,

712

Because I could not stop for Death—
He kindly stopped for me—
The Carriage held but just Ourselves—
And Immortality.

We slowly drove—He knew no haste
And I had put away
My labor and my leisure too,
For His Civility—

We passed the School, where Children strove
At Recess—in the Ring—
We passed the Fields of Gazing Grain—
We passed the Setting Sun—

Or rather—He passed Us—
The Dews drew quivering and chill—
For only Gossamer, my Gown—
My Tippet—only Tulle—

We paused before a House that seemed
A Swelling of the Ground—
The Roof was scarcely visible—
The Cornice—in the Ground—

Since then—'tis Centuries—and yet
Feels shorter than the Day
I first surmised the Horses' Heads
Were toward Eternity—

c. 1863

Their lessons scarcely done;
We passed the fields of gazing grain,
We passed the setting sun.

We paused before a house that seemed
A swelling of the ground;
The roof was scarcely visible,
The cornice but a mound.

Since then 'tis centuries; but each
Feels shorter than the day
I first surmised the horses' heads
Were toward eternity.

If the word "great" means anything in poetry, this poem is one of the greatest in the English language. The rhythm charges with movement the pattern of suspended action back of the poem. Every image is precise and, moreover, not merely beautiful, but fused with the central idea. Every image extends and intensifies every other. The third stanza especially shows Miss Dickinson's power to fuse, into a single order of perception, a heterogeneous series: the children, the grain, and the setting sun (time) have the same degree of credibility; the first subtly preparing for the last. The sharp *gazing* before *grain* instills into nature a cold vitality of which the qualitative richness has infinite depth. The content of death in the poem eludes explicit definition. He is a gentleman taking a lady out for a drive. But note the restraint that keeps the poet from carrying this so far that it becomes ludicrous and incredible; and note the subtly interfused erotic motive, which the idea of death has presented to most romantic poets, love being a symbol interchangeable with death. The terror of death is objectified through this figure of the genteel driver, who is made ironically to serve the end of Immortality. This is the heart of the poem: she has presented a typical Christian theme in its final irresolution, without making any final statements about it. There is no solution to the problem; there can be only a presentation of it in the full context of intellect and feeling. A construction of the human will, elaborated with all the abstracting powers of the mind, is put to the concrete test of experience: the idea of immortality is confronted with the fact of physical disintegration. We are not told what to think; we are told to look at the situation.

There was general agreement in this era about which of Dickinson's poems were most impressive. They were the "clean" (a favorite word with Blackmur), formally accomplished poems, such as "Because I could not stop for Death," "Safe in their Alabaster Chambers," and "Presentiment—is that long Shadow—on the Lawn—" that rewarded the New Critics' attention to form and their concentration on "the poem itself." (Their praise of Dickinson's precision was often the flipside of their relative silence about the sprawling meters and stanzas of Walt Whitman.) Blackmur called for a careful examination of the manuscripts in order to determine "whether a given item is a finished poem, an early version of a poem, a note for a poem, a part of a poem, or a prose exclamation." "No text will be certain," he wrote, "so long as the vaults at Amherst remain closed."

But once the vaults were opened, the text remained uncertain—and it is this very uncertainty that excites many critics today. Dickinson now seems most characteristic when most fragmentary in expression, most completely herself when most formally incomplete. If it is one of the major traits of Romantic art to blur the distinction between drafts, sketches, and exercises on the one hand and finished works on the other, Dickinson is a Romantic poet. We now know that even in what we assume to be final drafts she often left alternative words, as though she wanted her readers to choose. Thus she is, as the poet Adrienne Rich puts it, "equivocal to the end."

In the present period of Dickinson criticism, which began with the publication of the variorum edition of the poems in 1955 (restored to her own peculiar spellings, punctuation, and diction) and of the letters in 1958, the major achievements have been two. The first, which complements the restoration of the texts, is the great documentary retrieval of Dickinson's life, undertaken by Jay Leyda and all but completed by Richard Sewall. The cobwebs of legend have for the most part been swept away. A second achievement is feminist criticism of Dickinson, of which two works can be singled out as particularly fine. One is Ellen Moers's study of Dickinson as a woman writer, obsessed with other women writers, in her book *Literary Women*. The other is Adrienne Rich's extraordinary essay, "Vesuvius at Home," in which Rich tries to get at the source of Dickinson's creative depth and fury. (The chapter on Dickinson in *The Madwoman in the Attic*, by Sandra Gilbert and Susan Gubar, owes much to Rich's groundbreaking essay.) Feminist critics tend to stress the ways in which Dickinson resisted the difficulties of being a woman poet. They resemble the critics of the twenties and thirties in their sense of Dickinson as a heroic figure. One poem in particular has seemed crucial to feminist critics, and what follows is Rich's reading of it:

There is one poem which is the real "onlie begetter" of my thoughts here about Dickinson; a poem I have mused over, repeated to myself, taken into myself over many years. I

think it is a poem about possession by the daemon, about
the dangers and risks of such possession if you are a woman,
about the knowledge that power in a woman can seem de-
structive, and that you cannot live without the daemon
once it has possessed you. The archetype of the daemon as
masculine is beginning to change, but it has been real for
women up until now. But this woman poet also perceives
herself as a lethal weapon:

> My Life had stood—a Loaded Gun—
> In Corners—till a Day
> The Owner passed—identified—
> And carried me away—
>
> And now We roam in Sovereign Woods—
> And now We hunt the Doe—
> And every time I speak for Him—
> The Mountains straight reply—
>
> And do I smile, such cordial light
> Upon the Valley glow—
> It is as a Vesuvian face
> Had let its pleasure through—
>
> And when at Night—our good Day done—
> I guard My Master's Head—
> 'Tis better than the Eider-Duck's
> Deep Pillow—to have shared—
>
> To foe of His—I'm deadly foe—
> None stir the second time—
> On whom I lay a Yellow Eye—
> Or an emphatic Thumb—

> Though I than he—may longer live
> He longer must—than I—
> For I have but the power to kill,
> Without—the power to die—

Here the poet sees herself as split, not between anything so simple as "masculine" and "feminine" identity but between the hunter, admittedly masculine, but also a human person, an active, willing being, and the gun—an object, condemned to remain inactive until the hunter—the *owner*—takes possession of it. The gun contains an energy capable of rousing echoes in the mountains and lighting up the valleys; it is also deadly, "Vesuvian;" it is also its owner's defender against the "foe." It is the gun, furthermore, who *speaks for him*. If there is a female consciousness in this poem it is buried deeper than the images: it exists in the ambivalence toward power, which is extreme. Active willing and creation in women are forms of aggression, and aggression is both "the power to kill" and punishable by death. The union of gun with hunter embodies the danger of identifying and taking hold of her forces, not least that in so doing she risks defining herself—and being defined—as aggressive, as unwomanly, ("and now we hunt the Doe") and as potentially lethal. That which she experiences in herself as energy and potency can also be experienced as pure destruction. The final stanza, with its precarious balance of phrasing, seems a desperate attempt to resolve the ambivalence; but, I think, it is no resolution, only a further extension of ambivalence.

> Though I than he—may longer live
> He longer must—than I—
> For I have but the power to kill,
> Without—the power to die—

The poet experiences herself as loaded gun, imperious energy; yet without the Owner, the possessor, she is merely lethal. Should that possession abandon her—but the thought is unthinkable: "He longer *must* than I." The pronoun is masculine; the antecedent is what Keats called "The Genius of Poetry."

Criticism at its best is the effort to receive writers into the house of literature, to make it possible for readers to meet them there. The documentary retrieval of Dickinson's life and work, without which most of the recent criticism of her poetry would be unthinkable, was largely the work of Thomas Johnson, who edited the poems and letters, Jay Leyda, who helped with the editing and arranged the documents on which all future biographies would depend, and Richard Sewall, who wrote the standard life of the poet. This ongoing work shows to what extent we do not yet fully possess this poet. She eludes us still, as we try to give her a proper place to live in our literature. Readers will continue to make the pilgrimage to the Dickinson Homestead, to see where she lived her own life, and it seems fitting to conclude this account of her reception with Jay Leyda's verse essay about the Dickinson houses. The deed that he quotes is the actual deed of the Homestead.

A HOUSE TO BE BORN IN
An Essay in Biography

by Jay Leyda

The Deed: the west part of the home lot on which Samuel F.
Dickinson now dwells

> Early in eighteen thirty
> Samuel's fortunes foundered,
> Soon to sink in other people's debts
> And the politics
> Of his own too open self.
>
> Edward, the son who stuck,
> Tired of shifting annually
> His new wife and newer son,
> Bought and mortgaged that western half
> To prop his father and himself.
>
> The girl Edward married
> Brought with her dowry
> An infirm belief
> That everything and nothing
> Would take care of itself—
>
> But in her new half-house
> The morning her first daughter came,
> She kept the paper-hanger busy,
> Perhaps for the final time
> To assert her self.

the dwelling house in which he lives in said Amherst

> Within a landscape of gently graded proprieties,
> This village—this hive of abstraction—
> This cauldron of the concrete, boiling beneath its
>   broadcloth,
> Believing then and now its own aspect of peace.
> Warmth was suspect, and chill the habit,
> Yet gossip could joggle the steadiest cup of tea.

Beginning on the North side of the County road, in front of said dwelling house, at a point from which a line drawn parallel with the East and West sides of said dwelling house will run to the centre of the Front door

> The invisible line that runs to cut
> The closed door is blinder
> Than the three children brought
> Up and in and over the threshold,
> Their duties visibly outlined
> On a line drawn parallel
> To a past but present generation.
> The rules of safety were bound by walls.
>
> Outside—along the road—
> Waited all that mustn't
> Shouldn't and cannot.

and on the North side of said dwelling house the line begins at the west side of the west bed room & runs to the North line of the lot parallel with the sides of the house aforesaid & includes all the land in said lot West thereof

Ten years of half a house,
Ten years of half a childhood
For the surest of the three.
Now the girls' girlhood is to change
The venue of its blood and dream
To a house less arctic,
West of the prized bricked hillock,
A wooden, looser box on Pleasant Street,
Just over the graveyard's many boxes,
Already housing friends
Who played on the same lawns and ivory keys,
Made happy by the same old rhymes and cookies.

Also the west front room & chamber over it

Returning to the rigid pile of brick,
This west and front and upper compartment
Was given to her, and she to it.

Intervals of risk and care abroad,
Embraced by Springfield,
Patted by Monson, pained by Boston,
Mired in Middletown—
Always to return
A little blurred of step,
A little sharpened in gaze,
Bearing loads of raw stuffs
For the alchemy of her upper room.

all the west part of the said house called the Office

Sold from under Samuel,
In Edward's turn, sold too,

But now regained—both halves,
In a triumph darkly
Yellow and brown
Outside and in,
Proof and evidence of mastery,
Of Honorable Esquire—
The house again divides.

A son can wish,
But he will bargain, too,
So this son anchored
Hard by the home pier,
Left his sisters fifty yards behind,
Married his father's choice;
Set into his new house
A few bricks from the old house,
Just for bad luck.

& half meaning the west half of the back chamber over the bed
room with the entries south of the same connected therewith

Other rooms draw in their bridges
On the tortured pause of sleep,
But the west front chamber
Offers its wakened chairs
To hosts, summoned and unsummoned,
Bearing concepts, delights, and agonies.

Amongst them in her room,
All exits shut—tight—
All entries open—wide—
Paved with lamp-wick,
Pencil, Weston's Linen (1876),

Or any handy scrap of passing paper:
The margins of some kindness from a puzzled neighbor,
The verso of some condescension or grocery list,
The waiting spaces of a coming or going envelope—
On these emerged the words
To soften the mortar
Between the bastion's bricks,
And reach the outside air.
Through the earliest morning
The women on their way to the hat factory
See another woman just closing her night's work,
Smiling from the west front upstairs window.

with the Common right of the front lower & chamber entries

Rights too common and accessible
To the encroaching worldly,
Trailing in its robed wake
The real foe's lies,
His screened brutalities,
So often greeted and invited
By sister and pseudo-sister—
Miles below,
An abyss away.

the west half of the Garret

Up here the last whiteness rounds
Within the knees of hills
On every flowing silent side;
Below, the memory of a garden,
Leaving small green footprints

94

Through a child's house of glass
That clings but slopes away
From father's walls.

the cellar under the west front room under the office part & the
west part of the North side of the large cellar, as far east as the
brick pillar standing in the cellar

Down here the last spring sends down
Probing roots to a darker level,
Beneath the doubts of surface;
A mind must have a pillar
To lean its summer tools against—
The life of work well begun,
The beginner ready for rest.

together with the Cider house and horse barn.

The last intoxications scattered behind
To jewel the prophet's cold poetic waters,
The procession can pass
Through front and rear of a grandly open barn;
Borne on six shoulders,
Swept through May's grasses,
Washed in the light of the sun,
The visitor arrives and is housed.

Poems

*Some of the poems in this selection are among the best known of
Dickinson's 1,775 poems. Others are less familiar. Every editor would
choose differently, but this offering is not entirely eccentric. Most of
these poems exemplify certain emphases of the Introduction—
especially those about landscape, animals, love, death, and thought.
The poems are numbered according to Thomas Johnson's
standard edition, with approximate dates of composition, and are
arranged chronologically.*

These are the days when Birds come back—
A very few—a Bird or two—
To take a backward look.

These are the days when skies resume
The old—old sophistries of June—
A blue and gold mistake.

Oh fraud that cannot cheat the Bee—
Almost thy plausibility
Induces my belief.

Till ranks of seeds their witness bear—
And softly thro' the altered air
Hurries a timid leaf.

Oh Sacrament of summer days,
Oh Last Communion in the Haze—
Permit a child to join.

Thy sacred emblems to partake—
Thy consecrated bread to take
And thine immortal wine!

c. 1859

Wild Nights—Wild Nights!
Were I with thee
Wild Nights should be
Our luxury!

Futile—the Winds—
To a Heart in port—
Done with the Compass—
Done with the Chart!

Rowing in Eden—
Ah, the Sea!
Might I but moor—Tonight—
In Thee!

c. 1861

258

There's a certain Slant of light,
Winter Afternoons—
That oppresses, like the Heft
Of Cathedral Tunes—

Heavenly Hurt, it gives us—
We can find no scar,
But internal difference,
Where the Meanings, are—

None may teach it—Any—
'Tis the Seal Despair—
An imperial affliction
Sent us of the Air—

When it comes, the Landscape listens—
Shadows—hold their breath—
When it goes, 'tis like the Distance
On the look of Death—

c. 1861

280

I felt a Funeral, in my Brain,
And Mourners to and fro
Kept treading—treading—till it seemed
That Sense was breaking through—

And when they all were seated,
A Service, like a Drum—
Kept beating—beating—till I thought
My Mind was going numb—

And then I heard them lift a Box
And creak across my Soul
With those same Boots of Lead, again,
Then Space—began to toll,

As all the Heavens were a Bell,
And Being, but an Ear,
And I, and Silence, some strange Race
Wrecked, solitary, here—

And then a Plank in Reason, broke,
And I dropped down, and down—
And hit a World, at every plunge,
And Finished knowing—then—

c. 1861

288

I'm Nobody! Who are you?
Are you—Nobody—Too?
Then there's a pair of us!
Don't tell! they'd advertise—you know!

How dreary—to be—Somebody!
How public—like a Frog—
To tell one's name—the livelong June—
To an admiring Bog!

c. 1861

322

There came a Day at Summer's full,
Entirely for me—
I thought that such were for the Saints,
Where Resurrections—be—

The Sun, as common, went abroad,
The flowers, accustomed, blew,
As if no soul the solstice passed,
That maketh all things new—

The time was scarce profaned, by speech—
The symbol of a word
Was needless, as a Sacrament,
The Wardrobe—of our Lord—

Each was to each The Sealed Church,
Permitted to commune this—time—
Lest we too awkward show
At Supper of the Lamb.

The Hours slid Fast—as Hours will,
Clutched tight, by greedy hands—
So faces on two Decks, look back,
Bound to opposing lands—

And so when all the time had leaked,
Without external sound
Each bound the Other's Crucifix—
We gave no other Bond—

Sufficient troth, that we shall rise—
Deposed—at length, the Grave—
To that new Marriage,
Justified—through Calvaries of Love—

c. 1861

341

After great pain, a formal feeling comes—
The Nerves sit ceremonious, like Tombs—
The stiff Heart questions was it He, that bore,
And Yesterday, or Centuries before?

The Feet, mechanical, go round—
Of Ground, or Air, or Ought—
A Wooden way
Regardless grown,
A Quartz contentment, like a stone—

This is the Hour of Lead—
Remembered, if outlived,
As Freezing persons, recollect the Snow—
First—Chill—then Stupor—then the letting go—

c. 1862

375

The Angle of a Landscape—
That every time I wake—
Between my Curtain and the Wall
Upon an ample Crack—

Like a Venetian—waiting—
Accosts my open eye—
Is just a Bough of Apples—
Held slanting, in the Sky—

The Pattern of a Chimney—
The Forehead of a Hill—
Sometimes—a Vane's Forefinger—
But that's—Occasional—

The Seasons—shift—my Picture—
Upon my Emerald Bough,
I wake—to find no—Emeralds—
Then—Diamonds—which the Snow

From Polar Caskets—fetched me—
The Chimney—and the Hill—
And just the Steeple's finger—
These—never stir at all—

c. 1862

441

This is my letter to the World
That never wrote to Me—
The simple News that Nature told—
With tender Majesty

Her Message is committed
To Hands I cannot see—
For love of Her—Sweet—countrymen—
Judge tenderly—of Me

c. 1862

465

I heard a Fly buzz—when I died—
The Stillness in the Room
Was like the Stillness in the Air—
Between the Heaves of Storm—

The Eyes around—had wrung them dry—
And Breaths were gathering firm
For that last Onset—when the King
Be witnessed—in the Room—

I willed my Keepsakes—Signed away
What portion of me be
Assignable—and then it was
There interposed a Fly—

With Blue—uncertain stumbling Buzz—
Between the light—and me—
And then the Windows failed—and then
I could not see to see—

c. 1862

520

I started Early—Took my Dog—
And visited the Sea—
The Mermaids in the Basement
Came out to look at me—

And Frigates—in the Upper Floor
Extended Hempen Hands—
Presuming Me to be a Mouse—
Aground—upon the Sands—

But no Man moved Me—till the Tide
Went past my simple Shoe—
And past my Apron—and my Belt
And past my Bodice—too—

And made as He would eat me up—
As wholly as a Dew
Upon a Dandelion's Sleeve—
And then—I started—too—

And He—He followed—close behind—
I felt His Silver Heel
Upon my Ankle—Then my Shoes
Would overflow with Pearl—

Until We met the Solid Town—
No One He seemed to know—
And bowing—with a Mighty look—
At me—The Sea withdrew—

c. 1862

526

To hear an Oriole sing
May be a common thing—
Or only a divine.

It is not of the Bird
Who sings the same, unheard,
As unto Crowd—

The Fashion of the Ear
Attireth that it hear
In Dun, or fair—

So whether it be Rune,
Or whether it be none
Is of within.

The "Tune is in the Tree—"
The Skeptic—showeth me—
"No Sir! In Thee!"

c. 1862

561

I measure every Grief I meet
With narrow, probing, Eyes—
I wonder if It weighs like Mine—
Or has an Easier size.

I wonder if They bore it long—
Or did it just begin—
I could not tell the Date of Mind—
It feels so old a pain—

I wonder if it hurts to live—
And if They have to try—
And whether—could They choose between—
It would not be—to die—

I note that Some—gone patient long—
At length, renew their smile—
An imitation of a Light
That has so little Oil—

I wonder if when Years have piled—
Some Thousands—on the Harm—
That hurt them early—such a lapse
Could give them any Balm—

Or would they go on aching still
Through Centuries of Nerve—
Enlightened to a larger Pain—
In Contrast with the Love—

The Grieved—are many—I am told—
There is the various Cause—
Death—is but one—and comes but once—
And only nails the eyes—

There's Grief of Want—and Grief of Cold—
A sort they call "Despair"—
There's Banishment from native Eyes—
In sight of Native Air—

And though I may not guess the kind—
Correctly—yet to me
A piercing Comfort it affords
In passing Calvary—

To note the fashions—of the Cross—
And how they're mostly worn—
Still fascinated to presume
That Some—are like My Own—

c. 1862

609

I Years had been from Home
And now before the Door
I dared not enter, lest a Face
I never saw before

Stare stolid into mine
And ask my Business there—
"My Business but a Life I left
Was such remaining there?"

I leaned upon the Awe—
I lingered with Before
The Second like an Ocean rolled
And broke against my ear—

I laughed a crumbling Laugh
That I could fear a Door
Who Consternation compassed
And never winced before.

I fitted to the Latch
My Hand, with trembling care
Lest back the awful Door should spring
And leave me in the Floor—

Then moved my Fingers off
As cautiously as Glass
And held my ears, and like a Thief
Fled gasping from the House—

c. 1872

613

They shut me up in Prose—
As when a little Girl
They put me in the Closet—
Because they liked me "still"—

Still! Could themself have peeped—
And seen my Brain—go round—
They might as wise have lodged a Bird
For Treason—in the Pound—

Himself has but to will
And easy as a Star
Abolish his Captivity—
And laugh—No more have I—

c. 1862

657

I dwell in Possibility—
A fairer House than Prose—
More numerous of Windows—
Superior—for Doors—

Of Chambers as the Cedars—
Impregnable of Eye—
And for an Everlasting Roof
The Gambrels of the Sky—

Of Visitors—the fairest—
For Occupation—This—
The spreading wide my narrow Hands
To gather Paradise—

c. 1862

741

Drama's Vitallest Expression is the Common Day
That arise and set about Us—
Other Tragedy

Perish in the Recitation—
This—the best enact
When the Audience is scattered
And the Boxes shut—

"Hamlet" to Himself were Hamlet—
Had not Shakespeare wrote—
Though the "Romeo" left no Record
Of his Juliet,

It were infinite enacted
In the Human Heart—
Only Theatre recorded
Owner cannot shut—

c. 1863

764

Presentiment—is that long Shadow—on the Lawn—
Indicative that Suns go down—

The Notice to the startled Grass
That Darkness—is about to pass—

c. 1863

793

Grief is a Mouse—
And chooses Wainscot in the Breast
For His Shy House—
And baffles quest—

Grief is a Thief—quick startled—
Pricks His Ear—report to hear
Of that Vast Dark—
That swept His Being—back—

Grief is a Juggler—boldest at the Play—
Lest if He flinch—the eye that way
Pounce on His Bruises—One—say—or Three—
Grief is a Gourmand—spare His luxury—

Best Grief is Tongueless—before He'll tell—
Burn Him in the Public Square—
His Ashes—will
Possibly—if they refuse—How then know—
Since a Rack couldn't coax a syllable—now.

c. 1863

812

A Light exists in Spring
Not present on the Year
At any other period—
When March is scarcely here

A Color stands abroad
On Solitary Fields
That Science cannot overtake
But Human Nature feels.

It waits upon the Lawn,
It shows the furthest Tree
Upon the furthest Slope you know
It almost speaks to you.

Then as Horizons step
Or Noons report away
Without the Formula of sound
It passes and we stay—

A quality of loss
Affecting our Content
As Trade had suddenly encroached
Upon a Sacrament.

c. 1864

861

Split the Lark—and you'll find the Music—
Bulb after Bulb, in Silver rolled—
Scantily dealt to the Summer Morning
Saved for your Ear when Lutes be old.

Loose the Flood—you shall find it patent—
Gush after Gush, reserved for you—
Scarlet Experiment! Sceptic Thomas!
Now, do you doubt that your Bird was true?

c. 1864

872

As the Starved Maelstrom laps the Navies
As the Vulture teased
Forces the Broods in lonely Valleys
As the Tiger eased

By but a Crumb of Blood, fasts Scarlet
Till he meet a Man
Dainty adorned with Veins and Tissues
And partakes—his Tongue

Cooled by the Morsel for a moment
Grows a fiercer thing
Till he esteem his Dates and Cocoa
A Nutrition mean

I, of a finer Famine
Deem my Supper dry
For but a Berry of Domingo
And a Torrid Eye.

c. 1864

891

To my quick ear the Leaves—conferred—
The Bushes—they were Bells—
I could not find a Privacy
From Nature's sentinels—

In Cave if I presumed to hide
The Walls—begun to tell—
Creation seemed a mighty Crack—
To make me visible—

c. 1864

986

A narrow Fellow in the Grass
Occasionally rides—
You may have met Him—did you not
His notice sudden is—

The Grass divides as with a Comb—
A spotted shaft is seen—
And then it closes at your feet
And opens further on —

He likes a Boggy Acre
A Floor too cool for Corn—
Yet when a Boy, and Barefoot—
I more than once at Noon
Have passed, I thought, a Whip lash
Unbraiding in the Sun
When stooping to secure it
It wrinkled, and was gone—

Several of Nature's People
I know, and they know me—
I feel for them a transport
Of cordiality—

But never met this Fellow
Attended, or alone
Without a tighter breathing
And Zero at the Bone—

c. 1865

998

Best Things dwell out of Sight
The Pearl—the Just—Our Thought.

Most shun the Public Air
Legitimate, and Rare—

The Capsule of the Wind
The Capsule of the Mind

Exhibit here, as doth a Burr—
Germ's Germ be where?

c. 1865

1052

I never saw a Moor—
I never saw the Sea—
Yet know I how the Heather looks
And what a Billow be.

I never spoke with God
Nor visited in Heaven—
Yet certain am I of the spot
As if the Checks were given—

c. 1865

1129

Tell all the Truth but tell it slant—
Success in Circuit lies
Too bright for our infirm Delight
The Truth's superb surprise

As Lightening to the Children eased
With explanation kind
The Truth must dazzle gradually
Or every man be blind—

c. 1868

1138

A Spider sewed at Night
Without a Light
Upon an Arc of White.

If Ruff it was of Dame
Or Shroud of Gnome
Himself himself inform.

Of Immortality
His Strategy
Was Physiognomy.

c. 1869

1202

The Frost was never seen—
If met, too rapid passed,
Or in too unsubstantial Team—
The Flowers notice first

A Stranger hovering round
A Symptom of alarm
In Villages remotely set
But search effaces him

Till some retrieveless Night
Our Vigilance at waste
The Garden gets the only shot
That never could be traced.

Unproved is much we know—
Unknown the worst we fear—
Of Strangers is the Earth the Inn
Of Secrets is the Air—

To analyze perhaps
A Philip would prefer
But Labor vaster than myself
I find it to infer.

c. 1871

1212

A word is dead
When it is said,
Some say.

I say it just
Begins to live
That day.

c. 1872

1400

What mystery pervades a well!
That water lives so far—
A neighbor from another world
Residing in a jar

Whose limit none have ever seen,
But just his lid of glass—
Like looking every time you please
In an abyss's face!

The grass does not appear afraid,
I often wonder he
Can stand so close and look so bold
At what is awe to me.

Related somehow they may be,
The sedge stands next the sea—
Where he is floorless
And does no timidity betray

But nature is a stranger yet;
The ones that cite her most
Have never passed her haunted house,
Nor simplified her ghost.

To pity those that know her not
Is helped by the regret
That those who know her, know her less
The nearer her they get.

c. 1877?

1405

Bees are Black, with Gilt Surcingles—
Buccaneers of Buzz.
Ride abroad in ostentation
And subsist on Fuzz.

Fuzz ordained—not Fuzz contingent—
Marrows of the Hill.
Jugs—a Universe's fracture
Could not jar or spill.

c. 1877

1515

The Things that never can come back, are several—
Childhood—some forms of Hope—the Dead—
Though Joys—like Men—may sometimes make a Journey—
And still abide—
We do not mourn for Traveler, or Sailor,
Their Routes are fair—
But think enlarged of all that they will tell us
Returning here—
"Here!" There are typic "Heres"—
Foretold Locations—
The Spirit does not stand—
Himself—at whatsoever Fathom
His Native Land—

c. 1881

1540

As imperceptibly as Grief
The Summer lapsed away—
Too imperceptible at last
To seem like Perfidy—
A Quietness distilled
As Twilight long begun,
Or Nature spending with herself
Sequestered Afternoon—
The Dusk drew earlier in—
The Morning foreign shone—
A courteous, yet harrowing Grace,
As Guest, that would be gone—
And thus, without a Wing
Or service of a Keel
Our Summer made her light escape
Into the Beautiful.

c. 1865

1645

The Ditch is dear to the Drunken man
For is it not his Bed—
His Advocate—his Edifice?
How safe his fallen Head
In her disheveled Sanctity—
Above him is the sky—
Oblivion bending over him
And Honor leagues away.

c. 1885

Bibliography

In selecting materials for an introduction to Emily Dickinson, I could not hope to represent all the different views of her. The Introduction here has some of the ambitions of an "overview," but it comes to rest in a few subjects that seem to be particularly interesting today. My selection of passages regarding the reception of Dickinson's poetry may seem arbitrary. I did not look for a Marxist reading (are there any?), a psychoanalytic reading (there are many), a feminist or misogynist reading. I gave up trying to provide a history of how Dickinson has been read since the 1890s, offering instead a few readings that I thought were particularly fine—models of critical energy and excitement. I asked myself throughout what someone who knew little about Emily Dickinson (and most of what the "common reader" knows about her is inaccurate) would find most interesting.

I have plundered Richard Sewall's superb biography, *The Life of Emily Dickinson*, and have borrowed things here and there from many Dickinson critics. Some of these I have acknowledged in the text, but in an effort to keep scholarly apparatus at a minimum, many such debts must go unacknowledged. I do wish to thank Richard Sewall for his advice and encouragement.

Emily Dickinson's poems can be read in the three-volume variorum edition, *The Poems of Emily Dickinson* (Harvard, 1955), but they are more readily available in a reader's edition (*The Complete Poems of Emily Dickinson*) and in the standard selected poems, *Final Harvest* (both Little Brown). All three editions are edited by Thomas Johnson. The fascicle poems have been published in a two-volume facsimile edition edited by Ralph Franklin, *The Manuscript Books of Emily Dickinson*

(Harvard, 1981). In addition to the three-volume complete letters (Harvard, 1958) there is a *Selected Letters* (Harvard), both edited by Thomas Johnson.

Some of the books and essays I have found most helpful are also of interest to the general reader. Sewall's *The Life of Emily Dickinson* (Farrar, Straus and Giroux, 1974, two volumes; one-volume paperback, 1980), despite its length, is a good place to start. Jay Leyda's *The Years and Hours of Emily Dickinson* (Yale, 1960), if this regretably out-of-print work can be located, is a fascinating source for those interested in Dickinson's milieu. A fine short introduction to Dickinson's life and work is the chapter on her in Alfred Kazin's *An American Procession* (Knopf, 1984).

A great deal has been written on Dickinson and the tradition of women's literature. In addition to Adrienne Rich's essay, "Vesuvius at Home," first published in *Parnassus* in 1976, and the pages on Dickinson in Ellen Moers's *Literary Women* (Oxford, 1976), readers might look at the chapter on her in *The Madwoman in the Attic,* by Sandra Gilbert and Susan Gubar (Yale, 1979).

On the love affair of Dickinson's brother see Polly Longsworth's *Austin and Mabel* (Holt, 1984) and Peter Gay's *The Bourgeois Experience: Education of the Senses* (Oxford, 1984).

Among the best early essays on Dickinson are the classic ones by R.P. Blackmur, Allen Tate, Conrad Aiken, and Yvor Winters. The last three, as well as a later essay by Blackmur, are included in *Emily Dickinson: A Collection of Critical Essays*, edited by Richard Sewall (Prentice-Hall, 1963). To these can be added Richard Wilbur's "Sumptuous Destitution," also in the Sewall collection, and Northrop Frye's essay in *Fables of Identity* (Harcourt Brace Jovanovich, 1963).

Index of First Lines

Following the first lines of the poems are the poem numbers. The lines here do not reflect the exact punctuation or capitalization as they stand in the text. The pages on which they appear are at right.

INDEX OF FIRST LINES